HIGH SCHOOL SPELLING & VOCABULARY WORKBOOK

ACHIEVE HIGHER TEST SCORES WITH INTERACTIVE EXERCISES: VOCABULARY AND SPELLING HIGH SCHOOL WORKBOOK FOR GRADES 9-10

DR. FANATOMY
★★★★★

copyright@ dr. fanatomy 2024

All rights reserved. No part of this publication may be reproduced, distributed, or transmitted in any form or by any means, including photocopying, recording, or other electronic or mechanical methods, without the prior written permission of the publisher, except in the case of brief quotations embodied in critical reviews and certain other noncommercial uses permitted by copyright law.

This book is a work of non-fiction, and any resemblance to actual persons, living or dead, or actual events is purely coincidental.

The information and techniques described in this book are intended for educational and informational purposes only. The author and publisher shall not be held liable for any injury, damage, or loss arising from using or misusing the information presented in this book.

While every effort has been made to ensure the accuracy of the information contained within this book, the author and publisher make no warranties or representations express or implied, about the completeness, accuracy, reliability, suitability, or availability with respect to the contents of this book for any purpose. The use of any information provided in this book is at the reader's own risk.

DR. FANATOMY

Bonus Booklet For You!

With great pleasure, I warmly welcome you to purchase the book. Congratulations on stepping towards improving yourself and developing the skills necessary to thrive as a teenager and beyond.

Below is a surprise gift for you!

Download it from the link (or scan the QR code below)
https://bit.ly/TeeNavigationBonus

"29" LIFE SECRETS FOR TEENS YOU'LL ONLY DISCOVER WHEN YOU TURN 25!

DR. FANATOMY

TABLE OF CONTENTS

1. INTRODUCTION TO SPELLING AND VOCABULARY (Pg:4-8)

- Welcome Message
- The Importance of Strong Spelling and Vocabulary Skills
- Benefits for Academic Success
- Real-World Applications
- Common Spelling and Vocabulary Challenges
- Trivia Corner
- Activity Corner 1

2. BUILDING A STRONG VOCABULARY FOUNDATION (Pg:9-15)

- Understanding Vocabulary Levels
- Techniques for Vocabulary Acquisition
- Types of Context Clues
- Root Words, Prefixes, and Suffixes
- Trivia Corner
- Activity Corner 2

3. EFFECTIVE SPELLING STRATEGIES (Pg:16-22)

- Phonics and Spelling Patterns
- Spelling Rules and Exceptions
- Trivia Corner
- Activity Corner 3

4. VOCABULARY IN CONTEXT (Pg:23-29)

- Using Vocabulary in Sentences
- Synonyms, Antonyms, and Homophones
- Trivia Corner
- Activity Corner 4

5. ENHANCING VOCABULARY WITH READING (Pg: 30-40)

- Reading Strategies for Vocabulary Growth
- Annotating and Highlighting New Words
- Sample vocabulary for the different genres
- Science fiction words
- Fantasy words
- Historical Fiction words
- Mystery/Thriller words
- Classical Literature words
- Trivia Corner
- Activity Corner 5

6. WORD ROOTS, PREFIXES, AND SUFFIXES   (Pg: 41-48)

- *Understanding Word Roots*
- *Types of Roots*
- *Prefixes and Suffixes: Expanding Word Knowledge*
- *Trivia Corner*
- *Activity Corner 6*

7. ADVANCED SPELLING TECHNIQUES   (Pg: 49-53)

- *Spelling Complex Words*
- *Handling Multisyllabic Words*
- *Phonetic Approach*
- *Mnemonics and Memory Aids*
- *Visual Aids*
- *Trivia Corner*
- *Activity Corner 7*

8. LEVEL UP YOUR WRITING GAME   (Pg: 54-64)

- *Why Bother with Big Words?*
- *Word Power: Finding Your Super Vocabulary*
- *Make Your Essays and Reports Epic*
- *Redundancy and Wordiness: Keep it Simple, Stupid!*
- *Vocabulary for Every Occasion*
- *Essay*
- *Research Papers*
- *Literary Analysis*
- *Creative Writing*
- *Journaling and Reflective Writing*
- *Vocabulary for Other Subjects*
- *Additional Activities*
- *Trivia Corner*
- *Activity Corner 8*

9. MOST COMMON SPELLING MISTAKES   (Pg: 65-74)

- *Introduction*
- *Homophones*
- *Commonly Misspelled Words*
- *Words with Double Letters:*
- *Words with Tricky Vowel Combinations*
- *Words with Silent Letters*
- *Trivia Corner*
- *Activity Corner 9*

10. ACING THE VOCABULARY GAME IN EXAM (Pg: 75-82)

- *Techniques for Guessing the Correct Meaning*
- *Use Context Clues*
- *Analyze Word Parts (Morphology)*
- *Eliminate Incorrect Options*
- *Use Word Familiarity*
- *Check for Logical Fit*
- *Consider Connotations*
- *Tables and Visual Aids*
- *Trivia Corner*
- *Activity Corner 10*

ACTIVITY ANSWERS (Pg: 83 -91)

11. BUILD YOUR WORD BANK: VOCABULARY ESSENTIALS
(Pg: 92-100)

Vocabulary Improvement Groups
Group 1: Words from Latin Roots
Group 2: Words from Greek Roots
Group 3: Words with Positive Connotations
Group 4: Words with Negative Connotations
Group 5: Academic Words

Most Used Root Words from Different Languages
Table 1: Latin Roots
Table 2: Greek Roots
Table 3: French and Sanskrit Roots
Table 4 : German Roots
Table 5 : Old English Roots

12. MOST MISSPELLED WORDS & TRICKS TO REMEMBER (Pg: 101-103)

CONCLUSION (Pg: 104)

APPENDIX (Pg: 106-107)

- *Appendix- 1: Additional Resources*
- *Appendix- 2: Writing Prompts to Use New Vocabulary in Context*

1. Introduction to Spelling and Vocabulary

Welcome Message

Welcome to *"High School Spelling and Vocabulary Workbook: Achieve Higher Test Scores with Expert-Led Interactive Exercises for Grades 9-10."* "This workbook is designed to help you improve your spelling and vocabulary skills, essential for academic success and effective communication. We are thrilled to be on this journey with you, offering expert guidance and interactive exercises to make learning engaging and impactful. Let's dive in and begin building a strong foundation for your future achievements!"

The Importance of Strong Spelling and Vocabulary Skills

Benefits for Academic Success

Strong spelling and vocabulary skills are essential for academic success. Here are some key benefits:

- **Improved Reading Comprehension**: A robust vocabulary allows you to understand and interpret texts more effectively, making reading a more enjoyable and enriching experience. It keeps you engaged and interested in the material.

- **Enhanced Writing Skills:** Proper spelling and a diverse vocabulary are not just academic tools; they are practical skills that enable you to express your ideas clearly and persuasively in essays, reports, and other written assignments. They make you more prepared and competent in the real world.

- **Improved Test Scores**: Standardized tests, including the SAT and ACT, heavily emphasize vocabulary and spelling. Mastering these skills can significantly boost your test scores, opening doors to higher education and future opportunities.

- **Increased Confidence**: Knowing how to spell words correctly and use them appropriately boosts your confidence in both academic and social settings.

Real-World Applications :

Spelling and vocabulary skills are essential not only in the classroom but also in various real-world contexts.

- **Professional Communication:** Clear and accurate language is essential in the workplace, whether you are writing emails, reports, or presentations.

- **Compelling Storytelling**: Strong spelling skills and a rich vocabulary enhance your ability to captivate your audience, whether for creative writing or public speaking.

- **Daily Interactions:** Strong language skills improve your ability to communicate effectively and make a positive impression, whether in social media posts or casual conversations.

Common Spelling and Vocabulary Challenges

Typical Mistakes and Misconceptions

Many students struggle with certain aspects of spelling and vocabulary. Here are some common challenges:

- **Homophones**: Words that sound the same but have different meanings and spellings (e.g., "their," "there," "they're").

Homophone	Meaning	Example Sentence
Their	Possessive form	Their house is big.
There	Location	The book is over there.
They're	They are	They're going to the park.

- **Irregular Spelling Rules**: English has many exceptions to standard spelling rules. *Example: The rule "i before e except after c" does not apply in words like "science" and "weird."*

- **Word Usage**: Confusion about when to use certain words, especially those that are similar in meaning (e.g., "affect" vs. "effect").

Example:
- Affect (verb): The weather can affect your mood.
- Effect (noun): The effect of the new law was immediate.

- **Spelling Patterns**: Difficulty recognizing and applying common spelling patterns and rules.

Example: Silent letters, such as the "k" in "knight" or "b" in "doubt."

Trivia Corner

Let's test your knowledge with some fun trivia about the English language:

What is the longest word in the English dictionary?
- Answer: Pneumonoultramicroscopicsilicovolcanoconiosis.

Which word is the most frequently used in English writing?
- Answer: "The."

How many words are added to the English dictionary each year on average?
- Answer: Approximately 1,000 new words.

What is the shortest complete sentence in English?
- Answer: "I am."

Which English word has the most definitions?
- Answer: "Set," with over 430 different meanings.

🎯 ACTIVITY CORNER 1
Initial Spelling and Vocabulary Assessment

To begin, let's assess your current spelling and vocabulary skills. This will help you identify areas for improvement and set goals for this workbook.

1. Spelling Test: Write the correct spelling of the following words:

   1. Accommodation
   2. Necessary
   3. Environment
   4. Definitely
   5. Recommend
   6. Embarrassment
   7. Maintenance
   8. Rhythm
   9. Separate
   10. Occurrence

2. Vocabulary Test: Match the words with their definitions:

   1. **Exacerbate:**
      (a) To improve
      (b) To worsen
      (c) To examine

   2. **Benevolent:**
      (a) Kind-hearted
      (b) Unfriendly
      (c) Neutral

   3. **Ambiguous:**
      (a) Clear
      (b) Vague
      (c) Certain

   4. **Persevere:**
      (a) To give up
      (b) To continue
      (c) To pause

   5. **Candid**
      (a) Deceitful
      (b) Honest
      (c) Secretive

2. Building a Strong Vocabulary Foundation

Understanding Vocabulary Levels

Building a solid foundation involves recognizing the different vocabulary levels and progressively advancing from primary to advanced words.

Basic Vocabulary:

Basic vocabulary consists of commonly used words in daily conversations and basic writing, and it is essential for effective understanding and communication in English.

Examples:
- *Cat*
- *House*
- *Happy*
- *Run*
- *Friend*

Intermediate Vocabulary:

Intermediate vocabulary comprises more complex words commonly used in academic and formal communications. They require a more profound understanding and are less common in casual conversation.

Examples:
- *Benevolent*
- *Eloquent*
- *Persistent*
- *Ambiguous*
- *Frugal*

Advanced Vocabulary:

Advanced vocabulary consists of complex words used in specialized fields or advanced academic writing; mastering these words can significantly improve your communication skills and academic performance.

Examples:

- *Ubiquitous*
- *Magnanimous*
- *Ostentatious*
- *Perspicacious*
- *Quixotic*

Vocabulary Level	Example Words	Usage
Basic	Cat, House, Happy, Run, Friend	Daily conversations and basic writing
Intermediate	Benevolent, Eloquent, Persistent	Academic settings and formal communications
Advanced	Ubiquitous, Magnanimous, Ostentatious	Specialized fields and advanced writing

Techniques for Vocabulary Acquisition:

Effective techniques for acquiring and retaining new words are crucial for establishing a solid vocabulary base.

Context Clues:

Context clues are hints or information provided within a sentence or passage to help infer the meaning of an unfamiliar word. Knowing how to use context clues can significantly enhance your ability to learn new words naturally.

Example Sentence:

The benevolent teacher always helped students, showing kindness and generosity in every interaction.

Here, the words "kindness" and "generosity" provide context clues to understand that "benevolent" means kind-hearted or generous.

Types of Context Clues:

- **Definition Clues:** The word's meaning is given directly in the sentence. *Example: An arboreal animal like a monkey spends most of its life in trees.*

- **Synonym Clues**: A synonym of the word is used in the sentence. ***Example**: The garrulous woman was very talkative and couldn't stop chatting.*

- **Antonym Clues**: The sentence uses an antonym or word with an opposite meaning. For e***xample**, Mark is shy and reserved, unlike his gregarious brother, who loves socializing.*

- **Example Clues:** Examples are given to explain the word. ***Example:** Celestial bodies, such as the sun, moon, and stars, are fascinating to study.*

- **Inference Clues**: The word's meaning is inferred from the overall context of the sentence or passage. ***Example**: Despite the tumultuous storm, the captain remained calm, navigating through the chaos.*

Root Words, Prefixes, and Suffixes:

Understanding root words, prefixes, and suffixes can significantly enhance your vocabulary. They allow you to decode the meanings of unfamiliar words.

Root Words: Remember, a root word is the fundamental part of a word that conveys the main meaning. Knowing common root words can assist you in understanding many words with similar meanings, providing you with a strong foundation to enhance your vocabulary.

Examples:
- *"Dict" (**to say or speak**) -> Predict, Dictionary, Dictate*
- *"Cred" (**to believe**) -> Incredible, Credible, Credit*

Prefixes: A prefix is a group of letters added to the beginning of a word to change its meaning.

Examples:

- *"Un-" (not) -> Unhappy, Unfair, Uncertain*
- *"Re-" (again) -> Rewrite, Rebuild, Reconsider*

Suffixes: A suffix is a group of letters added to the end of a word to change its meaning or grammatical function.

Examples:
- *"-ful" (full of) -> Joyful, Helpful, Hopeful*
- *"-less" (without) -> Hopeless, Fearless, Tireless*

Technique	Definition	Example Words
Root Words	Basic part of a word carrying the main meaning	Dict (Predict, Dictionary)
Prefixes	Letters added to the beginning of a word	Un- (Unhappy, Unfair)
Suffixes	Letters added to the end of a word	-ful (Joyful, Helpful)

Trivia Corner

What is the longest word in English that can be typed using only the top row of letters on a QWERTY keyboard?
- *Answer: Typewriter*

Which word is the only one in English that contains three consecutive sets of double letters?
- *Answer: Bookkeeper*

What is the term for a word that means opposite to another word?
- *Answer: Antonym*

Which word is the longest palindrome in the English language?
- *Answer: Racecar*

What is the study of the origin and history of words called?
- *Answer: Etymology*

ACTIVITY CORNER 2

Activity Exercise: Building a Strong Vocabulary Foundation

1. What is a common technique for figuring out an unfamiliar word's meaning based on the surrounding words?

A) Using a thesaurus
B) Context clues
C) Memorizing definitions
D) Asking a friend

2. Which level of vocabulary includes words like "benevolent," "eloquent," and "persistent"?

A) Basic
B) Intermediate
C) Advanced
D) Expert

3. What is the root word in "reconsider"?

A) Re-
B) Con
C) Sid
D) Consider

4. What prefix means "not" and can be found in words like "unhappy" and "unbelievable"?

A) Re-
B) Un-
C) Pre-
D) Dis-

5. Which of the following suffixes means "full of"?

A) -ness
B) -ful
C) -able
D) -less

ACTIVITY CORNER 2

Activity Exercise: Building a Strong Vocabulary Foundation

6. In the sentence "The gregarious child made friends easily," what does "gregarious" mean?

A) Shy
B) Talkative
C) Sociable
D) Quiet

7. Which of these words is an example of an advanced vocabulary word?

A) House
B) Persistent
C) Magnanimous
D) Friend

8. What context clue directly defines a word within the sentence?

A) Synonym clue
B) Antonym clue
C) Inference clue
D) Definition clue

9. "Joyful" comprises which root word and suffix?

A) Joy and -ful
B) Joy and -less
C) Joy and -able
D) Joy and -ness

10. What is a common error when using context clues?

A) Using a dictionary
B) Ignoring surrounding text
C) Memorizing definitions
D) Asking a teacher

3. Effective Spelling Strategies

Phonics and Spelling Patterns

Phonics and spelling patterns are crucial for helping students understand how letters combine to create words. Mastering these patterns can significantly enhance spelling skills.

Common Phonetic Rules:
Short Vowel Sounds:

- *When a vowel is followed by a consonant, it usually has a short sound.*
- *Examples: cat, bed, sit, top, cut*

Long Vowel Sounds:

- *When a vowel is followed by a silent 'e' or is at the end of a syllable, it usually has a long sound.*
- *Examples: cake, bike, note, cute*

Consonant Blends:

- *Two or more consonants are blended, but each sound is still heard.*
- *Examples: bl (blue), tr (tree), sp (spot), cl (clap)*

Consonant Digraphs:

- *Two consonants come together to make one sound.*
- *Examples: ch (chicken), sh (shoe), th (think), ph (phone)*

Vowel Digraphs:

- *Two vowels come together to make one sound.*
- *Examples: ea (bread), oa (boat), ai (rain), ee (tree)*

Silent Letters:

- *Some letters in a word are not pronounced.*
- *Examples: knight, gnome, comb, wrist*

Spelling Rules and Exceptions

Learning common spelling rules and their exceptions can help students spell correctly and understand why some words deviate from the norms.

"I before E except after C" and Other Rules:

"I before E except after C":

- Examples: believe, field, friend (I before E)
- Exceptions: receive, deceive, weird, height (E before I after C or exceptions)

Doubling the Final Consonant:

- When adding a suffix to a one-syllable word ending in a single vowel and a single consonant, double the final consonant.
- Examples: run + ing = running, stop + ed = stopped
- Exceptions: open + ing = opening, visit + ed = visited

Dropping the Final E:

- Drop the final 'e' when adding a suffix beginning with a vowel.
- Examples: make + ing = making, bake + er = baker
- Exceptions: noticeable, courageous (words ending in 'ce' or 'ge')

Changing 'Y' to 'I':

- Change 'y' to 'i' when adding a suffix unless the suffix begins with 'i'.
- Examples: happy + ness = happiness, baby + s = babies
- Exceptions: play + ing = playing, joy + ful = joyful

Rule	Examples	Exceptions
I before E except after C	believe, field, friend	receive, deceive, weird
Doubling the Final Consonant	running, stopped	opening, visited
Dropping the Final E	making, baker	noticeable, courageous
Changing 'Y' to 'I'	happiness, babies	playing, joyful

Table: Common Phonetic Rules and Examples

Phonetic Rule	Example Words
Short Vowel Sounds	cat, bed, sit, top, cut
Long Vowel Sounds	cake, bike, note, cute
Consonant Blends	blue, tree, spot, clap
Consonant Digraphs	chicken, shoe, think, phone
Vowel Digraphs	bread, boat, rain, tree
Silent Letters	knight, gnome, comb, wrist

Sight Words and High-Frequency Words

Sight and high-frequency words are words that students should recognize without using decoding strategies. These words are commonly found in written text and often do not follow standard phonetic rules.

Examples of Sight Words:
- *the, to, he, she, we, was, they, you, are, have*

Examples of High-Frequency Words:
- *because, there, after, could, again, different, important, thought, through, together*

Sight Words	High-Frequency Words
the, to, he, she	because, there, after, could
we, was, they, you	again, different, important
are, have	thought, through, together

Trivia Corner

Fun Facts About Spelling

- **Set:** "Set" has many definitions, making it one of the most versatile words in English.

- **Queue:** The word "queue" is pronounced the same as "cue."

- Many English words come from Old English, **Latin**, and **Greek.**

- The word **"alphabet"** comes from the first two letters of the Greek alphabet, alpha and beta.

- The word "b**ookkee**per" has three sets of double letters.

- What is the only word in English that contains all five vowels in order? "F**a**c**e**t**io**us" contains all five vowels in order (a, e, i, o, u).

- The longest monosyllabic words in English are "screeched" and "strengths."

- **"Spoonerisms"** are phrases in which the initial sounds of words are swapped. A spoonerism is a linguistic phenomenon in which the initial consonants of two words are switched, such as saying "tease my ears" instead of "ease my tears." This term is named after Reverend William Archibald Spooner, famous for making these errors.

- The dot over the letters "i" and "j" is called a "tittle."

- **"Almost"** is the longest word, and all the letters are alphabetically ordered.

- **"Rhythm"** is the longest English word without a vowel.

ACTIVITY CORNER 3

Exercise 1: Fill in the Blanks with the Correct Spelling

1. The _____ (child) are playing in the park.
2. She is _____ (make) a cake for the party.
3. We _____ (receive) the package yesterday.
4. The _____ (play) is very joyful.
5. The _____ (big) storm caused damage.

Exercise 2: Match the Rule to the Example

1. Doubling the Final Consonant
A) making
B) babies
C) running

2. Dropping the Final E
A) friend
B) noticed
C) joyful

3. Changing 'Y' to 'I'
A) field
B) happiness
C) received

4. "I before E except after C"
A) believe
B) playing
C) noticeable

🎯 ACTIVITY CORNER 3

Trivia Corner

- **What is the longest word in English that doesn't repeat any letters?**
  Answer: "Uncopyrightable"

- **What is the most commonly misspelled word in the English language?**
  Answer: "Separate" (often misspelled as "separate")

- **What English word has the most definitions?**
  Answer: "Set"

- **What is the only word in English that ends with "mt"?**
  Answer: "Dreamt"

- **What is the shortest complete sentence in the English language?**
  Answer: "I am."

Exercise 3: Spelling Bee Practice

Instructions:

Spelling List Preparation:
- *Create a list of 20 challenging words from your recent lessons. Include a mix of basic, intermediate, and advanced words.*

Partner Up:
- *Pair up with a classmate or family member. Take turns pronouncing and spelling words from your list.*

Spelling Bee Practice:
- *Conduct a mock spelling bee. One person reads and uses the word in a sentence, and the other spells it. Switch roles after each word.*

4. Vocabulary in Context

Using Vocabulary in Sentences

Understanding Word Meaning and Usage

Understanding words' meaning and proper usage is essential for effectively incorporating vocabulary into sentences. This involves delving into strategies for deciphering word meanings and applying them appropriately in different contexts.

- **Context Clues**

Context clues help infer the meaning of unknown words by examining the surrounding text. Let's look at a few examples :

Examples:

Sentence: "The voracious reader finished the book in just one day."
Context Clue: The phrase "finished the entire book in just one day" helps to infer that "voracious" means eagerly approaching reading.

Sentence: "Despite the tumultuous weather, the soccer game continued as scheduled."
Context Clue: The phrase "despite the weather" and knowing the game continued despite it suggests "tumultuous" means stormy or chaotic.

Sentence: "She felt elated when she received her acceptance letter to her dream college."
Context Clue: The phrase "when she received her acceptance letter to her dream college" indicates that "elated" means extremely happy or overjoyed.

Sentence: "The magician's trick was so bewildering that the audience was completely confused."
Context Clue: The phrase "the audience was completely confused" helps to infer that "bewildering" means confusing or puzzling.

- **Word Parts**

Analyzing words by breaking them down into their roots, prefixes, and suffixes helps understand their meanings. For example, recognizing that "bio-" signifies life and "-logy" denotes the study of can help one comprehend that "biology" refers to the study of life.

Examples:

Word	Prefix	Meaning of Prefix	Root	Meaning of Root	Suffix	Meaning of Suffix	Overall Meaning
Unhappiness	un-	not	happy	state of being happy	-ness	state or quality of	The state of not being happy
Microscope	micro-	small	scope	instrument for viewing			An instrument used to view small objects
Antibiotic	anti-	against	bio-	life	-tic	pertaining to	A substance used to kill or inhibit bacteria
Geothermal	geo-	earth	therm	heat			Pertaining to the heat of the earth
Transcontinental	trans-	across	continent	large landmass	-al	pertaining to	Pertaining to or spanning across continents

- **Usage Examples**

Words can have different meanings based on context. For example, "set" can refer to a collection of items (a set of books), the act of placing something (set the table), or a group of repetitions in exercise (three sets of ten push-ups).

Examples:

Word	Context 1	Meaning 1	Context 2	Meaning 2	Context 3	Meaning 3
Set	A set of books	A collection of items	Set the table	The act of placing something	Three sets of ten push-ups	A group of repetitions in exercise
Light	The room is filled with light	Illumination	Light luggage	Not heavy	Light the candle	To ignite

- **Usage Examples *Continued*....**

Word	Context 1	Meaning 1	Context 2	Meaning 2	Context 3	Meaning 3
Break	Take a break from work	A pause or rest	Break the glass	To cause something to separate	Break a habit	To end or discontinue a behavior
Run	Go for a run in the park	To move swiftly on foot	Run a business	To manage or operate	Run the program	To execute or start
Point	The point of the pencil	The sharp end	Make a point in discussion	An argument or statement	Point at the screen	To direct attention by indicating

Synonyms, Antonyms, and Homophones

Understanding relationships between words enhances vocabulary skills. This section includes detailed explanations and examples to illustrate these concepts.

- **Synonyms**: Words with similar meanings. For example, "happy" and "joyful." Practice using synonyms in sentences to enrich your writing.
- **Antonyms**: Words with opposite meanings. For instance, "hot" and "cold." Practice exercises will help identify and use antonyms correctly.
- **Homophones**: Words that sound the same but have different meanings and spellings, such as "there," "their," and "they're." Examples and exercises will clarify these often-confusing words.

Concept	Example 1	Sentence 1	Example 2	Sentence 2	Example 3	Sentence 3
Synonyms	Happy - Joyful	She felt happy/joyful at the news.	Sad - Unhappy	He was sad/unhappy about the loss.	Fast - Quick	The fast/quick runner won the race.
Antonyms	Hot - Cold	The soup is hot/cold.	Big - Small	The big/small dog barked loudly.	Begin - End	The movie will begin/end soon.
Homophones	There - Their - They're	There is a cat. / Their car is new. / They're coming over.	To - Too - Two	I want to go to the park. / She is coming too. / I have two apples.	Your - You're	Is this your book? / You're amazing.

Trivia Corner

Word Origins

- **Sandwich:** The word "sandwich" is named after John Montagu, the 4th Earl of Sandwich. He popularized eating meat between two slices of bread so he could continue gambling without using a fork.

- **Panic:** Derived from the Greek god Pan, who was believed to cause sudden, irrational fear in humans.

- **Quarantine:** From the Italian word "quaranta," meaning forty. Ships suspected of carrying the plague were isolated for forty days.

Language Facts

- **Longest Word:**

The longest word in English is "pneumonoultramicroscopicsilicovolcanoconiosis," a lung disease caused by inhaling very fine silicate or quartz dust.

- **Words That Have Changed Meaning:**

Awful: Originally meant "full of awe" and was used as a term of admiration. Now, it means something very bad or unpleasant.

Nice: It once meant "silly" or "foolish" in the 14th century. Today, it means pleasant or agreeable.

- **Palindromes:**

Words or phrases that read the same backward and forward, such as "madam" or "racecar."

ACTIVITY CORNER 4
Activity: Vocabulary Games and Challenges

Activity 1: Fill-in-the-Blanks :

Complete the sentences using the correct vocabulary words: **arboretum, voracious, elated, cowered, bewildering, and tumultuous.**

1. The children were ____ when they heard they were going to Disneyland.
2. The puppy ____ in the corner during the loud fireworks.
3. Reading the entire series in a week shows she is a ____ reader.
4. The ____ weather didn't stop the parade from happening.
5. The new math concept was ____ to most of the students.
6. They visited the ____ to learn more about different tree species.

Activity 2 Multiple Choice Quiz :

Choose the correct answer for each question.

1. Which word means "extremely happy or overjoyed"?
a) Tumultuous
b) Bewildering
c) Elated
d) Cowered

2. Which word describes someone eager to approach an activity?
a) Voracious
b) Arboretum
c) Cowered
d) Tumultuous

3. What does "bewildering" mean?
a) A place with various trees and shrubs
b) Confusing or puzzling
c) Stormy or chaotic
d) Extremely happy

ACTIVITY CORNER 4

Activity: Vocabulary Games and Challenges

Activity 2 Multiple Choice Quiz :

Choose the correct answer for each question.

4. "Tumultuous" best describes:
a) Quiet and calm
b) Extremely happy
c) Stormy or chaotic
d) Eager to read

5. The word "cowered" means:
a) Crouched down in fear
b) Very eager to read
c) Stormy or chaotic
d) Confusing or puzzling

Activity 3 : Match the Following

Match the Following	Options
1. Synonym for "angry"	a) Bright
2. Synonym for "quick"	b) Furious
3. Antonym for "dark"	c) Decrease
4. Antonym for "increase"	d) Fast
5. Antonym for "happy"	e) Sad

5. Enhancing Vocabulary with Reading

30

Reading Strategies for Vocabulary Growth

Reading is a powerful tool for expanding vocabulary. This section focuses on strategies to make the most of reading to enhance your word knowledge.

Selecting Challenging Texts :

Choosing the right texts is crucial for vocabulary growth. Here's how to select and approach challenging texts:

- **Identify Your Level**: Choose texts slightly above your current reading level. For example, try a classic novel or an advanced non-fiction book if you're comfortable with high school literature.

- **Diverse Genres**: Explore various genres to encounter different vocabulary. For instance, reading science fiction can introduce specialized terms, while classic literature offers rich, descriptive language.

Genre	Examples	Vocabulary Focus
Fiction	"To Kill a Mockingbird," "1984"	Narrative and descriptive words
Non-Fiction	"Sapiens," "The Immortal Life of Henrietta Lacks"	Technical and factual terms
Poetry	Works by Emily Dickinson, Robert Frost	Figurative language and themes
Science Fiction	"Dune," "Neuromancer"	Speculative and technical terms

Annotating and Highlighting New Words :

Effective annotation and highlighting can help retain new vocabulary.

- **Highlighting:** Use a highlighter to mark unfamiliar words. For instance, in a passage from Pride and Prejudice, highlight words like "obsequious" and "rectitude" to look them up later.

Annotating: Write definitions or synonyms in the margins. For example, next to "ameliorate," you might write "improve" or "enhance."

Example:

- **Text Excerpt:** "His obsequious behavior towards the manager was evident to everyone in the office."
- **Annotation:** Obsequious = excessively eager to please; similar to "flattering" or "servile."

Word	Sentence Context	Definition
Obsequious	"His obsequious behavior towards the manager…"	Excessively eager to please
Ameliorate	"Efforts to ameliorate the situation were evident."	To make something better or improve

Annotating: Write definitions or synonyms in the margins. For example, next to "ameliorate," you might write "improve" or "enhance."

Example:

- **Text Excerpt:** "His obsequious behavior towards the manager was evident to everyone in the office."
- **Annotation:** Obsequious = excessively eager to please; similar to "flattering" or "servile."

Let's see the sample vocabulary for the different genres we read!

Science fiction

Word	Context Sentence	Root Word	Tips
Quantum	The scientist explained the principles of quantum physics to the class.	Latin quantus	Think of "quantity" to remember "quantum."
Nebula	The spaceship glided through a colorful nebula in the distant galaxy.	Latin nebula	Nebula sounds like "nebula"—think of "nebula" in space.
Hologram	They used a hologram to project the image of the alien planet.	Greek holos	"Holo-" means whole, so think of a whole image.
Cyborg	The hero was a cyborg with both human and robotic parts.	Greek cyber	Combine "cyber" and "organism" to remember.
Paradox	The time travel created a paradox that puzzled the scientists.	Greek para-	A paradox is a "pair" of opposing ideas.
Telepathic	She had a telepathic connection with her alien friend.	Greek tele-	"Tele-" means distance, so think of "distant thoughts."
Nanotechnology	Nanotechnology was crucial for repairing the spaceship.	Greek nano-	"Nano" means very small, like "nano-sized tech."
Extraterrestrial	The crew encountered an extraterrestrial species.	Latin extra-	"Extra" means beyond, so "beyond Earth."
Android	The android helped with daily tasks around the spaceship.	Greek andro-	Think of "android" as a "man-like" robot.
Galactic	They traveled across galactic distances in their spaceship.	Greek galaxy	"Galactic" relates to "galaxy" or large space.
Antimatter	Antimatter was used as a powerful energy source.	Greek anti-	"Anti-" means against, so think of "against matter."
Cyberspace	They navigated through cyberspace to find information.	Greek cyber	"Cyber" relates to computers, think "computer space."
Terraform	They planned to terraform the planet to make it habitable.	Latin terra	"Terraform" means to "make Earth-like."
Subspace	The ship entered a subspace to travel faster than light.	Latin sub-	"Sub-" means below, so think "below normal space."
Biometric	Biometric security ensured that only authorized personnel could enter.	Greek bio-	"Bio-" means life, think "life measurements."
Invasive	The alien species proved to be highly invasive.	Latin in-	"Invasive" means "inward-moving" or "intrusive."
Futuristic	The design of the city was distinctly futuristic.	Latin future	"Futuristic" relates to the "future" of design.
Hyperspace	The ship jumped into hyperspace to escape the enemy.	Greek hyper-	"Hyper-" means "beyond," so think "beyond normal space."

Fantasy

Word	Context Sentence	Root Word	Tips
Enchanted	The enchanted forest was filled with magical creatures.	Latin incantare	"Enchant" sounds like "chanted," think "chanted with magic."
Mystical	The mystical realm was hidden from the ordinary world.	Greek mystikos	"Mystical" sounds like "mystery," think "full of mystery."
Spellbound	The audience was spellbound by the wizard's performance.	Old English spell	"Spell" and "bound," think "bound by a spell."
Sorcery	The ancient art of sorcery was passed down through generations.	Latin sors	"Sorcery" sounds like "sorcerer," think "magical practice."
Potion	She brewed a potion to cure the king's illness.	Latin potio	"Potion" sounds like "pot," think "brewing in a pot."
Legendary	The legendary hero was known throughout the land.	Latin legendarius	"Legend" think "famous story," think "hero of a story."
Runes	The ancient runes glowed with magical energy.	Old Norse rún	"Runes" sounds like "ruins," think "ancient symbols."
Dragon	The dragon guarded its treasure fiercely.	Greek drakon	"Dragon" think "large, fire-breathing creature."
Elixir	The elixir granted eternal youth to whoever drank it.	Arabic al-iksir	"Elixir" sounds like "licks," think "potion to drink."
Knight	The knight rode valiantly into battle.	Old English cniht	"Knight" sounds like "night," think "medieval soldier."
Fey	The forest was inhabited by fey creatures who could enchant anyone.	Old English faie	"Fey" sounds like "fairy," think "magical beings."
Grimoire	The wizard's grimoire contained powerful spells.	Old French gramaire	"Grimoire" think "book of magic spells."
Chivalry	Chivalry was a code of conduct for the knights.	Old French chevalerie	"Chivalry" sounds like "chivalrous," think "knightly conduct."
Arcane	The arcane knowledge was only known to a few.	Latin arcanus	"Arcane" think "secret knowledge," think "mysterious."
Wyrm	The ancient wyrm slept deep beneath the mountains.	Old English wyrm	"Wyrm" sounds like "worm," think "dragon-like creature."
Goblin	The goblin hordes threatened the peace of the kingdom.	Middle English gobelin	"Goblin" think "mischievous creature."
Sanctuary	The sanctuary was a place of refuge and safety.	Latin sanctuarium	"Sanctuary" think "sacred place," think "safe haven."
Alchemy	The study of alchemy aimed to turn base metals into gold.	Arabic al-kimiya	"Alchemy" think "transforming materials," think "ancient chemistry."
Talisman	She carried a talisman for good luck.	Greek telesma	"Talisman" think "magical object," think "lucky charm."
Quest	The hero embarked on a quest to find the lost artifact.	Latin quaerere	"Quest" sounds like "question," think "search or adventure."

34

Historical Fiction

Word	Context Sentence	Root Word	Tips
Revolution	The French Revolution changed the course of history.	Latin revolutio	"Revolution" think "revolve," think "a turning point."
Empire	The Roman Empire stretched across Europe, Asia, and Africa.	Latin imperium	"Empire" sounds like "emperor," think "large kingdom."
Monarch	The monarch ruled with absolute power.	Greek monarkhos	"Monarch" think "one ruler," think "king or queen."
Crusade	The knight joined the Crusade to reclaim the Holy Land.	Latin crux	"Crusade" think "cross," think "religious war."
Renaissance	The Renaissance was a period of great cultural and artistic growth.	French renaissance	"Renaissance" think "rebirth," think "cultural revival."
Colonial	The colonial era saw the expansion of European powers into the Americas.	Latin colonia	"Colonial" think "colony," think "settlements."
Artifact	The archaeologists discovered an ancient artifact.	Latin arte factum	"Artifact" think "art" + "fact," think "man-made object."
Dynasty	The Ming Dynasty ruled China for nearly 300 years.	Greek dynasteia	"Dynasty" think "family rule," think "long-lasting reign."
Medieval	Medieval castles were built to withstand sieges.	Latin medium aevum	"Medieval" think "middle ages," think "old times."
Chivalry	Chivalry was a code of conduct for knights in the Middle Ages.	Old French chevalerie	"Chivalry" think "knightly conduct," think "honor."
Feudal	The feudal system structured medieval society.	Latin feodum	"Feudal" think "feud," think "land-based hierarchy."
Guild	The blacksmith belonged to a guild that regulated trade.	Old English gild	"Guild" sounds like "gilded," think "trade group."
Armistice	The armistice ended the hostilities between the warring nations.	Latin arma	"Armistice" think "arms" + "still," think "peace agreement."
Prohibition	Prohibition banned the sale of alcohol in the 1920s.	Latin prohibere	"Prohibition" think "prohibit," think "ban."
Abolition	The abolition of slavery was a significant moment in history.	Latin abolere	"Abolition" think "abolish," think "end of slavery."
Conquest	The Norman Conquest of England in 1066 changed the country's history.	Latin conquestare	"Conquest" think "conquer," think "takeover."
Reformation	The Reformation led to significant changes in the Christian church.	Latin reformatio	"Reformation" think "reform," think "religious change."
Industrial	The Industrial Revolution brought about technological advancements.	Latin industria	"Industrial" think "industry," think "machines and factories."
Treaty	The Treaty of Versailles ended World War I.	Latin tractatus	"Treaty" think "treat," think "formal agreement."
Legion	The Roman legion was a formidable military unit.	Latin legio	"Legion" sounds like "legend," think "large army."

Mystery/Thriller

Word	Context Sentence	Root Word	Tips
Alibi	She provided an alibi to prove she was elsewhere during the crime.	Latin alibi	"Alibi" sounds like "I'll be," think "where I'll be."
Suspect	The detective questioned the main suspect in the case.	Latin suspectare	"Suspect" think "suspicious," think "person under suspicion."
Clue	The clue found at the scene led them to the suspect.	Middle English cleue	"Clue" think "piece of information," think "hint."
Evidence	The evidence collected was crucial for the trial.	Latin evidentia	"Evidence" think "proof," think "something visible."
Interrogate	The officer had to interrogate the witness for more details.	Latin interrogare	"Interrogate" think "question aggressively," think "inquiry."
Motivation	The detective needed to find the motivation behind the crime.	Latin motivus	"Motivation" think "reason," think "motive."
Perpetrator	The perpetrator was finally caught after months of investigation.	Latin perpetrare	"Perpetrator" think "person who did it," think "doer of crime."
Forgery	The document was identified as a forgery by the experts.	Latin forgiare	"Forgery" think "fake," think "false document."
Blackmail	The victim received a blackmail letter demanding money.	Old English blæc + mælum	"Blackmail" think "threat," think "extortion."
Accomplice	The thief had an accomplice who helped in the heist.	Latin complicare	"Accomplice" think "helper in crime," think "partner."
Cipher	They needed to break the cipher to decode the message.	Arabic sifr	"Cipher" think "code," think "secret writing."
Dossier	The agent reviewed the dossier before proceeding with the case.	French dossier	"Dossier" think "file," think "collection of documents."
Infiltrate	The spy had to infiltrate the enemy organization.	Latin infiltrare	"Infiltrate" think "enter secretly," think "sneak in."
Conspiracy	They uncovered a conspiracy to overthrow the government.	Latin conspirare	"Conspiracy" think "secret plan," think "plot."
Stakeout	The police set up a stakeout to catch the criminal in the act.	Old English staca + utan	"Stakeout" think "surveillance," think "watching closely."
Double-cross	He was double-crossed by his partner in crime.	English double + cross	"Double-cross" think "betray," think "deceive."
Disguise	The detective wore a disguise to blend in.	Old French desguiser	"Disguise" think "change appearance," think "hide true identity."
Fingerprint	They found a fingerprint on the weapon.	English finger + print	"Fingerprint" think "unique mark," think "identification."
Anonymous	The tip came from an anonymous source.	Greek anonymos	"Anonymous" think "without a name," think "unknown."
Interception	The interception of the message prevented the crime.	Latin interceptio	"Interception" think "catching," think "stopping midway."

Classical Literature

Word	Context Sentence	Root Word	Tips
Allegory	The novel was an allegory for the struggle between good and evil.	Greek allegoria	"Allegory" sounds like "all" + "story," think "hidden meaning."
Soliloquy	Hamlet's soliloquy reveals his innermost thoughts.	Latin solus + loqui	"Soliloquy" think "solo" + "speech," think "alone on stage."
Epic	The Odyssey is an epic that recounts the adventures of Odysseus.	Greek epos	"Epic" think "long poem," think "grand tale."
Tragedy	Romeo and Juliet is a classic tragedy that ends in the death of both lovers.	Greek tragodia	"Tragedy" think "tragic," think "sad story."
Metaphor	The poet used a metaphor to describe the storm as an angry giant.	Greek metaphora	"Metaphor" think "figure of speech," think "comparison."
Allusion	The novel's title is an allusion to a line from Shakespeare.	Latin alludere	"Allusion" sounds like "illusion," think "reference."
Irony	It was ironic that the fire station burned down.	Greek eironeia	"Irony" think "opposite of expected," think "unexpected twist."
Paradox	The paradox of freedom is that it often involves constraint.	Greek paradoxos	"Paradox" think "contradiction," think "two opposing ideas."
Protagonist	The protagonist of the story faced many challenges.	Greek protagonistes	"Protagonist" think "main character," think "hero."
Antagonist	The antagonist plotted to overthrow the protagonist.	Greek antagonistes	"Antagonist" think "opponent," think "villain."
Foreshadow	The dark clouds foreshadowed the trouble ahead.	Old English for- + sceadwian	"Foreshadow" think "hint," think "predict."
Theme	The theme of the novel revolves around the conflict between fate and free will.	Greek thema	"Theme" think "central idea," think "main subject."
Apostrophe	The poet used apostrophe to address the absent lover directly.	Greek apostrophos	"Apostrophe" think "addressing someone absent," think "direct speech."
Euphemism	Using 'passed away' instead of 'died' is a euphemism.	Greek euphemismos	"Euphemism" think "mild expression," think "softer term."
Hyperbole	The author's use of hyperbole made the character's abilities seem superhuman.	Greek hyperbole	"Hyperbole" think "exaggeration," think "overstatement."
Symbolism	The green light in The Great Gatsby is a symbol of hope.	Greek symbolon	"Symbolism" think "symbol," think "representation."
Oxymoron	The phrase 'deafening silence' is an oxymoron.	Greek oxymoron	"Oxymoron" think "contradictory terms," think "opposite words together."
Satire	The novel is a satire that criticizes societal norms.	Latin satira	"Satire" think "humor with criticism," think "mockery."
Personification	The wind whispered secrets through the trees, a perfect example of personification.	Latin persona	"Personification" think "human traits to non-humans," think "animate."

Trivia Corner

- The average English speaker knows around 20,000 words.
- Shakespeare introduced over 1,700 new words to the English language.
- Reading just six books a year can increase your vocabulary by 88%.
- The human brain can store around 50,000 words.
- Learning a new word daily can increase your vocabulary by over 3,000 words yearly.
- The word "dictionary" comes from the Latin word "dictionarium," meaning "book of words."
- The average person uses about 7,000 different words in everyday speech.
- Reading fiction can improve your emotional intelligence.
- People who read regularly tend to have higher IQs.
- Reading can reduce stress levels.
- Just six minutes of reading can reduce stress by up to 68%.
- Reading improves concentration and focus.
- Reading stimulates the imagination.
- Reading can increase empathy and understanding of others.
- People who read often have better sleep quality.
- Reading can expand your knowledge and worldview.
- Reading can improve your writing skills.
- Lifelong learners are often avid readers.
- The average person reads about 4 books a year.
- Reading aloud can improve pronunciation and fluency.
- The first book ever printed was the Gutenberg Bible.
- The human brain processes information faster when reading than when listening.
- Reading can help you develop critical thinking skills.
- "Eye" is the only word with a letter in its name. It's looking right at you!
- There are only two words in the English language that end in "-gry": angry and hungry. Sounds like someone's in a mood!

ACTIVITY CORNER 5

Activity 1: Multiple Choice Questions

1. **Which of the following is NOT a benefit of enhancing vocabulary through reading?**
a) Improved cognitive functions
b) Increased empathy
c) Decreased retention of information
d) Greater understanding of context

2. **Which of the following can reading fiction enhance?**
a) Empathy
b) Vocabulary retention
c) Analytical thinking
d) All of the above

3. **What is one effective method for retaining new vocabulary encountered while reading?**
a) Ignoring new words
b) Using a vocabulary notebook
c) Skipping difficult passages
d) Only reading genres you are comfortable with

4. **Why is reading aloud beneficial for vocabulary enhancement?**
a) It makes reading faster
b) It reinforces pronunciation and retention
c) It helps to memorize entire books
d) It reduces the need for context understanding

5. **What type of learning occurs when readers pick up new words naturally while following a story?**
a) Intentional learning
b) Contextual learning
c) Incidental learning
d) Repetitive learning

Activity 2: Match the Words with Their Definitions

1) Allegory   2) Soliloquy   3) Metaphor   4) Hyperbole   5) Irony

a) A long speech by a character alone on stage
b) A story, poem, or picture that can be interpreted to reveal a hidden meaning
c) The expression of one's meaning by using language that normally signifies the opposite
d) An exaggerated statement or claim not meant to be taken literally
e) A figure of speech that involves an implied comparison

Activity 3: True or False

1. Reading only one genre will provide the same vocabulary enhancement as reading multiple genres. **(True/False)**
2. Vocabulary acquisition through reading often requires conscious effort to memorize new words. **(True/False)**
3. Reading fiction does not contribute to cognitive benefits. **(True/False)**
4. Associating new words with personal experiences can aid retention and recall. **(True/False)**
5. Encountering new words multiple times in different contexts helps solidify understanding. **(True/False)**

Activity 4: Fill in the Blanks

1. Engaging with different genres can significantly expand one's _____.

2. Words learned in _____ through reading are often remembered better.

3. Reading texts aloud can help reinforce vocabulary learning through better retention and _____.

4. Keeping a _____ while reading can be an effective tool for learning new words.

5. Repetition and _____ are key in vocabulary building.

6. Word Roots, Prefixes, and Suffixes

41

Understanding Word Roots :

Introduction

Words are the building blocks of language, and understanding their structure can significantly enhance your vocabulary. Word roots are the core elements that form the foundation of countless English words. By grasping the meaning of common roots, you'll unlock the ability to decipher unfamiliar terms and expand your word power.

Types of Roots

Body-Related Roots

Root	Meaning	Examples	Explanation
cardi-	Heart	Cardiology, Cardiac, Cardiogram	"Cardiology" is the study of the heart.
derm-	Skin	Dermatology, Epidermis, Hypodermic	"Dermatology" is the study of skin.
dent-	Tooth	Dentist, Dental, Denture	A "dentist" is a doctor for teeth.
neur-	Nerve	Neurology, Neuron, Neurotransmitter	"Neurology" is the study of nerves.
oste-	Bone	Osteopathy, Osteoporosis, Osteology	"Osteopathy" is a type of medicine focusing on bones and muscles.

Example: The word "neurology" combines the Greek root "neur" (nerve) and "logy" (study of), meaning the study of nerves.

Science and Nature Roots

Root	Meaning	Examples	Explanation
bio-	Life	Biology, Biography, Biodegradable	"Biology" is the study of life.

Science and Nature Roots

Root	Meaning	Examples	Explanation
geo-	Earth	Geography, Geology, Geothermal	"Geography" is the study of the earth's surface.
hydr-	Water	Hydration, Dehydrate, Hydroelectric	"Hydration" means maintaining water in the body.
therm-	Heat	Thermometer, Thermostat, Thermal	A "thermometer" measures heat.
astro-	Star	Astronomy, Astronaut, Astrophysics	"Astronomy" is the study of stars and planets.

Example: The word "biology" combines the Greek roots "bio" (life) and "logy" (study of), meaning the study of life.

Communication and Knowledge Roots

Root	Meaning	Examples	Explanation
dict-	Speak	Dictate, Dictionary, Prediction	A "dictionary" is a book of words and their meanings.
graph-	Write	Autograph, Biography, Telegraph	An "autograph" is a person's written signature.
phon-	Sound	Telephone, Phonograph, Symphony	A "telephone" is a device for communicating sound over distances.
scrib-	Write	Describe, Manuscript, Inscription	To "describe" means to write down details about something.
vis-	See	Vision, Visible, Television	"Vision" refers to the ability to see.

Example:

The word "television" combines the Greek root "tele" (far) and the Latin root "vis" (see), meaning seeing something from afar.

Prefixes and Suffixes: Expanding Word Knowledge

Common Prefixes:

Prefix	Meaning	Examples	Explanation
anti-	Against	Antisocial, Antibacterial, Antidote	"Antibacterial" means against bacteria.
dis-	Not/Opposite	Disagree, Disappear, Dislike	"Disappear" means to not be visible.
inter-	Between	International, Interact, Intercept	"International" means between nations.
mis-	Wrongly	Misunderstand, Misplace, Mislead	"Misunderstand" means to understand wrongly.
pre-	Before	Predict, Prepare, Prehistoric	"Predict" means to say before something happens.
re-	Again	Rewrite, Replay, Rebuild	"Rewrite" means to write again.
sub-	Under/Below	Submarine, Subtract, Subconscious	"Submarine" is a vessel that operates underwater.
trans-	Across/Through	Transport, Transfer, Translate	"Transport" means to carry across.
un-	Not	Unhappy, Unbelievable, Unusual	"Unhappy" means not happy.
under-	Below/Less Than	Underestimate, Underwater, Undergo	"Underwater" means below the water.

Example:

The word "submarine" combines the prefix "sub-" (under) with the root "marine" (sea), meaning a vessel that operates underwater.

Common Suffixes

Suffix	Meaning	Examples	Explanation
-able	Can be done	Comfortable, Portable, Breakable	"Comfortable" means can be comforted.
-ful	Full of	Joyful, Helpful, Careful	"Joyful" means full of joy.

Common Suffixes :

Suffix	Meaning	Examples	Explanation
-able	Can be done	Comfortable, Portable, Breakable	"Comfortable" means can be comforted.
-ful	Full of	Joyful, Helpful, Careful	"Joyful" means full of joy.
-less	Without	Hopeless, Fearless, Useless	"Hopeless" means without hope.
-ly	Characteristic of	Quickly, Softly, Happily	"Quickly" means in a quick manner.
-ment	Action/Process	Enjoyment, Achievement, Amendment	"Enjoyment" means the process of enjoying.
-ness	State of	Happiness, Kindness, Darkness	"Happiness" means the state of being happy.
-ous	Full of	Joyous, Dangerous, Continuous	"Dangerous" means full of danger.
-tion	Act/Process	Celebration, Creation, Organization	"Creation" means the process of creating.
-ive	Having the nature of	Active, Creative, Massive	"Active" means having the nature of activity.
-ology	Study of	Biology, Sociology, Geology	"Biology" means the study of life.

Example:

The word "happiness" combines the suffix "-ness" (state of) with the root "happy," meaning the state of being happy.

Understanding word roots, prefixes, and suffixes can significantly enhance your vocabulary and spelling skills. By breaking down words into their basic components, you can better understand their meanings and remember their spellings. Keep practicing, and soon you'll find that your ability to decipher new words improves dramatically!

Trivia Corner

- Did you know that the word "television" comes from the Greek word "tele" (far) and the Latin word "visio" (sight)?

- Fun Fact: The word "alphabet" comes from the first two letters of the Greek alphabet, "alpha" and "beta."

- Historical Tidbit: "salary" comes from "salarium," which in ancient Rome referred to the money given to soldiers to buy salt.

- Word Origin: The word "lunatic" comes from the Latin "lunaticus," meaning "moonstruck," because it was once believed that the moon influenced mental health.

- Etymology Insight: The word "school" comes from the Greek "schole," which originally meant "leisure" or "free time," as studying was considered a leisurely activity.

- Word Trivia: The prefix "pseudo-" means false or fake. So, "pseudonym" means a false name, commonly used by authors who want to hide their identity.

- Language Fun: The root "chrono-" means time. Therefore, "chronology" studies time and the order of events.

- Root Exploration: The root "phobia" means fear. Words like "arachnophobia" (fear of spiders) and "claustrophobia" (fear of confined spaces) are derived from this root.

- Prefix Insight: The prefix "retro-" means backward. So, "retrospective" means looking back at past events.

- Suffix Fun Fact: The suffix "-cracy" means rule or government. Therefore, "democracy" means government by the people.

🎯 ACTIVITY CORNER 6

Activity 1: Identify the Root

Identify the root word in each of the following words:

1. Audible
2. Biology
3. Predict
4. Transportation
5. Television
6. Dermatology
7. Submarine
8. Hydration
9. Manuscript
10. Astronaut

Activity 2: Matching Prefixes and Suffixes

Match the prefixes and suffixes with their meanings:

1. Anti- a) Before
2. Dis- b) Against
3. -ful c) Without
4. -less d) Not
5. Pre- e) Full of
6. Sub- f) Under/Below
7. -ment g) Action/Process
8. -ness h) State of
9. -ive i) Having the nature of
10. Inter- j) Between

47

Activity 3: Create New Words

Using the given prefixes and suffixes, create new words:

1. Un- + known = _____
2. Inter- + national = _____
3. Care + -ful = _____
4. Happy + -ness = _____
5. Celebrate + -tion = _____
6. Danger + -ous = _____
7. Write + -ive = _____
8. Geology + -ist = _____
9. Joy + -ous = _____
10. Comfort + -able = _____

Activity 4: Creating Word Trees

Creating word trees is a great way to visualize how words are formed and related. Let's make a word tree for the root "bio" (life).

Step-by-Step Guide:

1. Start with the root word "bio" in the center.
2. Draw branches to form words using prefixes and suffixes.
3. Write a sentence using each new word.

Example Word Tree:

```
                    bio
                   / | \
           biologist  biology  biodegradable
              /         |           \
      A biologist    Biology    Biodegradable materials
      studies life.  is the     break down
                     study of life. naturally.
```

Use the following roots and create your word tree:

Root Options:
1. geo (earth)
2. scrib (write)
3. Tele (far)

48

7. Advanced Spelling Techniques

Introduction :

Mastering spelling, enhancing memory, and engaging in learning through advanced techniques, exercises, and activities can be challenging, particularly with complex, multisyllabic words. This section is designed to provide the tools needed to conquer these challenges.

Spelling Complex Words

Handling Multisyllabic Words

Multisyllabic words can be tricky, but breaking them into manageable parts can make spelling easier. Here are some strategies to tackle these words effectively.

Syllable Breakdown: Divide words into syllables to simplify spelling. Understanding how words are constructed helps you remember their structure.

Examples:

- *Incredible: in-cred-i-ble*
- *Unbelievable: un-be-liev-a-ble*
- *International: in-ter-na-tion-al*

Word	Syllable Breakdown
Responsibility	re-spon-si-bil-i-ty
Incomprehensible	in-com-pre-hen-si-ble
Misunderstanding	mis-un-der-stand-ing

Phonetic Approach

Pronounce words slowly and clearly to hear each syllable. This technique helps associate the sounds with the correct letters.

Examples:

- *Phenomenon: phe-nom-e-non*
- *Articulation: ar-tic-u-la-tion*

Word	Phonetic Breakdown
Encyclopedia	en-cy-clo-pe-di-a
Hippopotamus	hip-po-pot-a-mus

Mnemonics and Memory Aids

Mnemonics are memory aids that help you remember complex information. They can be particularly useful for spelling.

Examples: Common Mnemonics

- *Because **B**ig **E**lephants **C**an **A**lways **U**nderstand **S**mall **E**lephants*
- *Rhythm: **R**hythm **H**elps **Y**our **T**wo **H**ips **M**ove*

Word	Mnemonic
Ne**cess**ary	One **C**ollar and Two **S**leeves are Necessary
Sepa**rat**e	There is a rat in separate

Visual Aids

Creating visual associations can help you remember the spelling of difficult words. Drawing a picture or imagining a scenario related to the word can reinforce your memory.

Examples:

Word	Visual Aid Description
Accommodate	Two rooms (two 'c's) and two beds (two 'm's) in a house.
Separate	A big rat standing between the letters 'a' and 'r'.
Necessary	A shirt with one collar and two sleeves.
Vacuum	A vacuum cleaner hose forming the shape of two 'u's.
Embarrassment	A blushing face with double 'r' for redness and two hands covering the face (double 's').
Rhythm	A heart beating in rhythm with no vowel between 'rh' and 'th'.

Trivia Corner

- **Fun Fact**: The word "queue" is the only word in English still pronounced the same way when the last four letters are removed.
- **Historical Tidbit**: The word "alphabet" originates from the first two letters of the Greek alphabet, "alpha" and "beta."
- **Word Origin**: The word "disaster" comes from the Italian "disastro," which means "bad star," referring to the belief that unfavorable astrological positions caused calamities.
- **Etymology Insight**: The word "salary" comes from the Latin word "salarium," which means "money given to soldiers to buy salt."

🎯 ACTIVITY CORNER 7

Activity 1: Correct Spelling Quiz

Instructions: Choose the correct word spelling for each question from the four options.

1. Which is the correct spelling?
 a) Accommodate b) Accommodate c) Acommodate d) Accomadate

2. Which is the correct spelling?
 a) Misunderstanding b) Missunderstanding c) Misunderstnding d) Misundrestanding

3. Which is the correct spelling?
a) Enviromentally b) Environmentaly c) Environmentally d) Enviornmentally

4. Which is the correct spelling?
a) Comitee b) Committe c) Committee d) Comittee

5. Which is the correct spelling?
 a) Millenium b) Milennium c) Millennium d) Millennum

Activity Set 2: Match the Following Mnemonics

Instructions: Match each word with the correct mnemonic.

Mnemonics:

1. Embarrassment
2. Millennium
3. Guarantee
4. Entrepreneur
5. Committee

a) Every New Tree Reaches Exceptional Peaks, Realizing Every New Unique Resource
b) My Illogical Little Lizard Enjoys New Neat Ice-cream Under Moonlight
c) Giant Unicorns Always Run Around Never Tearing Everything Else
d) Cats Often Meet Mice In The Tea Room Eating Everything
e) Emma Makes Bears And Rats Run Away Scared, Sometimes Emma Naps Too

8. Level Up Your Writing Game

Having a strong vocabulary is essential for effective communication. It allows you to express your thoughts clearly and shape your ideas precisely. For high school students, a rich vocabulary is especially important. It's the foundation for academic success, improved critical thinking, and clear self-expression. Let's uncover how an extensive vocabulary can enhance your writing in various styles.

Why Bother with Big Words?

Imagine your writing is a pizza. The crust (structure) is important, but the toppings (words) make it amazing. Big words are special toppings that take your writing from ordinary to extraordinary.

You've mastered the basics. Now, it's time to make your writing shine! Let's dive into the world of awesome words.

- **Impress your readers**: Show off your knowledge and make them think, "Wow, this person knows their stuff!"
- **Express yourself better**: Some ideas need a specific word to hit the mark.
- **Sound smarter**: Yep, it's true! Using the right words can make you sound super intelligent.

Word Power: Finding Your Super Vocabulary

So, how do you find these magical words?

- **Read like crazy**: Books, magazines, even cereal boxes – soak up those words!
- **Use a thesaurus:** Need a synonym for "good"? Your thesaurus is your new best friend.
- **Play word games**: Crossword puzzles and Scrabble – fun and a sneaky way to learn new words.

Example Time!

- Basic: "I really like that movie."
- Advanced: "I was utterly enthralled by that film."

Make Your Essays and Reports Epic

Your essays and reports are your chance to shine. Use your word power to make them awesome!

- **Choose words that fit**: Use strong, persuasive words for arguments, clear and informative words for explaining things, and vivid words for storytelling.
- **Avoid repetition**: Don't say the same thing twice. It's boring!
- **Be concise:** Get to the point. Don't use ten words when five will do.

Example Alert!

- *Basic: "Dogs are good pets."*
- *Advanced: "Canines are loyal and affectionate companions."*
- *Why it's better: "Canines" is more specific, and "loyal and affectionate" paints a better picture.*

Redundancy and Wordiness: Keep it Simple, Stupid!

Repeating yourself or using too many words is like adding extra cheese to your pizza – it can be overwhelming!

Redundancy:

- Saying the same thing twice.
- **Example**: "very unique" (unique means one of a kind, so "very" is unnecessary)

Wordiness:

- Using too many words to say something simple.
- *Example: "In order to" can often be replaced with "to."*

Common Word	Advanced Vocabulary
Big	Enormous
Smart	Intelligent
Good	Excellent
Help	Assist
Change	Transform

Vocabulary for Every Occasion

Your words can change depending on what you're writing.

(A) Essay (Part)

(1) Argumentative

- **Before:** "The school should have a longer lunch break. This will help students to relax and eat properly."

- **After:** "Extending the duration of lunch breaks will significantly enhance students' well-being, allowing them ample time to relax and consume their meals adequately."

Explanation:

- **Before**: The language is simple and lacks depth.

- **After**: Words like "extending," "duration," "significantly enhance," "well-being," and "adequately" add sophistication and clarity.

(2) Expository

Before: "Photosynthesis is how plants make food. It is important for their growth."

After: "Photosynthesis, the process by which plants synthesize food, is crucial for their growth and survival."

Explanation:

- **Before:** Basic explanation.
- **After:** Detailed and informative, using terms like "synthesize" and "crucial."

(3) Narrative

Before: "I went to the beach. It was nice and sunny."

After: "I visited the beach, where the sun bathed the golden sands in a warm, inviting glow."

Explanation:
- Before: Simple description.
- After: Vivid imagery with phrases like "bathed the golden sands" and "inviting glow."

(4) Persuasive

Before: "We should recycle more. It helps the environment."

After: "Increasing our recycling efforts is imperative for environmental conservation and sustainability."

Explanation:

- Before: Basic argument.
- After: Compelling and urgent with words like "imperative" and "sustainability."

(B) Research Papers

Objective: Present detailed, factual information on a specific topic.

- **Academic Words:** Use formal, precise language.
    - **Example:** Instead of "showed," use "demonstrated."

- **Examples:**
    - **Basic:** "The experiment showed that plants need light to grow. Without light, they don't grow well."
    - **Advanced:** "The experiment demonstrated that light is essential for plant growth, as the absence of light significantly hampers their development."

(C) Literary Analysis

Objective: Analyze and interpret a piece of literature.

- **Analytical Words:** Use words that express deep analysis.
    - Example: Instead of "the main character is sad," use "the protagonist's profound melancholy."

- **Examples:**
    - **Basic**: "The main character is sad because he lost his job."
    - **Advanced:** "The protagonist's profound melancholy stems from his sudden unemployment."

(D) Creative Writing

Objective: Create engaging and imaginative stories or poems.

- **Imaginative Words**: Use creative and figurative language.
    - **Example**: Use metaphors, similes, and personification.

- **Examples:**
    - Basic: "The dragon was big and scary."
    - Advanced: "The dragon loomed large and menacing, its fiery breath scorching the ground beneath."

(E) Journaling and Reflective Writing

Objective: Express personal thoughts and experiences.

- **Honest Words:** Use words that reflect your true feelings.
    - **Example:** Instead of "good," use "exceptionally delightful."

- **Examples:**
    - **Basic:** "Today was a good day. I felt happy."
    - **Advanced:** "Today was exceptionally delightful; I felt overwhelming joy."

(F) Vocabulary for Other Subjects

(1) Science

Objective: Explain scientific concepts clearly and accurately.
- **Scientific Words:** Use precise and technical terms.
    - **Examples:**
        - **Basic:** "The results of the lab were good. We learned a lot."
        - **Advanced:** "The lab results were remarkable, providing significant insights."

(2) History

Objective: Describe historical events and their significance.
- **Analytical Words:** Use words that express importance and impact.
    - **Examples:**
        - **Basic:** "The historical event was important. It changed things a lot."
        - **Advanced:** "The historical event was pivotal, catalyzing substantial changes."

(3) Social Studies

Objective: Discuss social issues and their effects on society.
- **Descriptive Words:** Use words that emphasize importance and depth.
    - **Examples:**
        - **Basic:** "Social issues are a big deal. They affect many people."
        - **Advanced:** "Social issues are paramount, impacting numerous individuals profoundly."

(4) Maths

Objective: Describe mathematical concepts and problem-solving steps.

- **Precise Words:** Use accurate and clear language.
    - Examples:
        - **Basic:** "The math problem was hard. I found a way to solve it."
        - **Advanced:** "The mathematical problem was challenging, but I devised an effective solution."

(G) Additional Activities

(1) Digital Writing

Objective: Write engaging content for digital platforms.

- **Engaging Words:** Use words that attract and hold attention.
    - Examples:
        - **Basic:** "Blogging is fun. You can share your ideas with others."
        - **Advanced:** "Blogging is an enjoyable platform for disseminating your thoughts to a wider audience."

(2) Collaborative Writing

Objective: Work with others to create a cohesive piece of writing.

- **Teamwork Words**: Use words that emphasize cooperation and success.
    - Examples:
        - **Basic**: "Group projects can be hard. Working together helps."
        - **Advanced**: "Collaborative projects can be challenging, but teamwork facilitates success."

(3) Portfolio Development

Objective: Professionally showcase your best work.

- **Professional Words**: Use words that highlight quality and excellence.
    - Examples:
        - **Basic**: "Creating a portfolio shows your best work."
        - **Advanced:** "Curating a portfolio highlights your exemplary work."

Trivia Corner

- **Most Common Word**: The most frequently used word in English is "the." It appears in about 5% of all English texts.

- **New Words**: The English language adds approximately 1,000 new words every year, reflecting changes in technology, culture, and society.

- **Shakespeare's Influence**: William Shakespeare is credited with coining or popularizing over 1,700 words in the English language, including "bedroom," "swagger," and "hurry."

- Palindrome Fun: A palindrome is a word that reads the same forward and backward. Examples include "racecar," "level," and "radar."

- Longest Palindrome: The longest single-word palindrome in English is "tattarrattat," coined by James Joyce in his novel "Ulysses" to imitate the sound of a knock on the door.

- Etymology Fascination: The word "etymology" comes from the Greek word "etymon," meaning "true sense," and "logia," meaning "study." It's the study of the origin of words and how their meanings have changed over time.

- Homophones Galore: English has many homophones—words that sound the same but have different meanings and spellings. Examples include "to," "two," and "too" or "their," "there," and "they're."

- Diverse Origins: English borrows words from many languages. For example, "algebra" comes from Arabic, "ballet" from French, "piano" from Italian, and "kangaroo" from an Australian Aboriginal language.

- Word of the Year: Every year, dictionaries like Oxford and Merriam-Webster select a "Word of the Year" based on its significance and popularity. Recent examples include "climate emergency" (2019) and "vaccine" (2021).

🎯 ACTIVITY CORNER 8

Activity 1: Vocabulary Challenge: Choose the Correct Word

Below is a paragraph with **two-word options in parentheses**. Your task is to select the correct word based on vocabulary and spelling. Good luck!

High school can be a(n) (exciting/exsiting) time, filled with opportunities for personal (growth/grouth) and academic (development/devlopment). Students are encouraged to (participate/partisapate) in various activities to (enhance/inhance) their skills. Whether it's joining a club, (pursuing/persewing) a hobby, or (volunteering/volenteering), there are many ways to (engage/ingage) in the school community.

Effective communication is crucial, and expanding your (vocabulary/vocabularry) can significantly (improve/impove) your (writing/writting) and speaking abilities. Reading books, (exploring/expolring) new words, and playing word games are excellent methods to (enrich/inrich) your language skills. Remember to always (proofread/proofreed) your work to avoid (common/commen) spelling errors.

In addition, learning to use (advanced/advansed) vocabulary in your essays can make your arguments more (persuasive/perswasive) and your explanations clearer. It's not just about (sounding/saounding) smarter; it's about being precise and (concise/consice) in your communication. So, take the time to (expand/expaned) your vocabulary, and watch your writing (transform/transforrm) from good to (exceptional/exceptionel).

Activity 2: Find the Errors

Below is a paragraph containing vocabulary and spelling errors. Your task is to identify and correct them. Good luck!

High school is a crusial time in a student's life, filled with many oppurtunities for learning and grouth. It is important to nuture your skills and knoledge during these years. Participating in extracuricular activities can greatly inritch your high school experience. Effective comunication is key to sucsess in both academic and social settings. Always remember to proofreed your work to catch any spelling or grammatical errors. Using a tesaurus can help you find synonims to enhance your vocabulary. By being dilligant and paying attention to detail, you can make the most of your high school years and prepare for a brigt future.

9. Most Common Spelling Mistakes

Introduction

Welcome to Chapter 9: Most Common Spelling Mistakes!

As high school students, you're constantly juggling various assignments, from essays and reports to creative writing and exams. Amid all this writing, it's easy for spelling errors to sneak in, affecting the clarity and professionalism of your work.

Spelling might seem like a small detail, but it plays a big role in how your writing is perceived. Misspelling words can make your arguments seem less convincing and your stories less engaging. In this chapter, we'll tackle some of the most common spelling mistakes that high school students make, and provide simple tips to help you remember the correct spellings.

We've categorized these mistakes into several common types:

- **Words with Silent Letters**: Some words contain letters that aren't pronounced. For example, in the word "castle," the "t" is silent. Recognizing these silent letters can help you spell words correctly and understand their pronunciation better.

- **Commonly Confused Words**: Many words sound similar but have different spellings and meanings. For instance, "affect" and "effect" are often mixed up. Knowing the distinctions between these words can improve your writing precision.

- **Homophones**: These words sound the same but are spelled differently and have different meanings, such as "there" and "their." Understanding homophones can help you use the correct word in the right context.

- **Words with Commonly Misspelled Prefixes and Suffixes**: Prefixes and suffixes can change the meaning of a word and sometimes lead to spelling errors. For example, "definately" is a common misspelling of "definitely."

- **Commonly Misspelled Words**: Some words are frequently misspelled due to their complexity or unusual spelling patterns. Words like "accommodate" and "recommend" often trip people up.

Homophones:

Homophones are words that sound the same but have different meanings and spellings. It's easy to mix them up in writing.

Incorrect Spelling	Correct Spelling	Trick to Remember
Their	There	"Their" shows possession, "there" refers to a place.
They're	Their	"They're" means "they are."
There	They're	"There" means a place.
Your	You're	"You're" means "you are."
You're	Your	"Your" shows possession.
Its	It's	"It's" means "it is."
It's	Its	"Its" shows possession.
To	Too	"Too" means also or excessively.
Too	Two	"Two" is the number 2.
Two	To	"To" is a direction or preposition.
Hear	Here	"Hear" means listening.
Here	Hear	"Here" means this place.
Weather	Whether	"Weather" is about climate.
Whether	Weather	"Whether" means if.
Affect	Effect	"Affect" is an action, "effect" is a result.
Effect	Affect	Remember "cause and effect."
Which	Witch	"Which" is for choices, "witch" is Halloween.
Witch	Which	"Which" asks questions, "witch" is spooky.
Right	Write	"Right" is correct, "write" is to jot down.

Commonly Misspelled Words :

These are words that are often spelled incorrectly due to tricky letter combinations or irregular spellings.

Incorrect Spelling	Correct Spelling	Trick to Remember
Definately	Definitely	"Definite-ly" is the base word.
Seperate	Separate	There's 'a rat' in 'separate'.
Neccessary	Necessary	One "c" and two "s"s in necessary.
Accomodate	Accommodate	Two "c"s and two "m"s in accommodate.
Recieve	Receive	"i" before "e" except after "c."
Occured	Occurred	Double "c" and double "r."
Wierd	Weird	"Weird" breaks the "i before e" rule.
Untill	Until	Only one "l" in until.
Beleive	Believe	"i" before "e" except after "c."
Committment	Commitment	Only one "t" in commitment.
Tommorrow	Tomorrow	One "m" in tomorrow.
Suprise	Surprise	"Surprise" has "r" after "u."
Foward	Forward	"For-ward" is the base word.
Goverment	Government	Remember the "n" in government.
Independant	Independent	Ends with "ent," not "ant."
Priviledge	Privilege	Only one "d" in privilege.
Publically	Publicly	Only one "l" in publicly.
Restuarant	Restaurant	"Restau-rant" is the base word.
Seperately	Separately	There's 'a rat' in 'separate-ly'.

Words with Double Letters:

These are words that students often misspell because they either add or omit extra letters.

Incorrect Spelling	Correct Spelling	Trick to Remember
Ocured	Occurred	Double "c" and double "r."
Tomorow	Tomorrow	One "m," two "r"s in tomorrow.
Acommodate	Accommodate	Two "c"s and two "m"s in accommodate.
Apear	Appear	Double "p" in appear.
Acess	Access	Double "c" in access.
Posession	Possession	Double "s" in possession.
Collage	College	Double "l" in college.
Comittment	Commitment	Only one "t" in commitment.
Acommodate	Accommodate	Two "c"s and two "m"s in accommodate.
Millenium	Millennium	Double "l" and double "n" in millennium.
Allot	A lot	"A lot" is two words.
Adress	Address	Double "d" in address.
Begining	Beginning	Double "n" in beginning.
Persue	Pursue	Only one "s" in pursue.
Proffesional	Professional	Double "s" in professional.
Asistent	Assistant	Double "s" in assistant.
Belive	Believe	"i" before "e" except after "c."
Embarras	Embarrass	Double "r" and double "s" in embarrass.
Recomend	Recommend	Double "m" in recommend.
Ocurred	Occurred	Double "c" and double "r" in occurred.

Words with Tricky Vowel Combinations :

These words often confuse students because the vowel combinations don't follow the usual rules.

Incorrect Spelling	Correct Spelling	Trick to Remember
Recieve	Receive	"i" before "e" except after "c."
Beleive	Believe	"i" before "e" except after "c."
Feirce	Fierce	"i" before "e" except after "c."
Freind	Friend	"Friend" has "i" before "e."
Hieght	Height	"e" before "i" after "h."
Nintey	Ninety	"Ninety" follows "nine" rule.
Peice	Piece	"i" before "e" except after "c."
Rythm	Rhythm	No "e" in rhythm.
Seige	Siege	"i" before "e" except after "c."
Tatoo	Tattoo	Double "t" and double "o" in tattoo.
Theif	Thief	"i" before "e" except after "c."
Vacinne	Vaccine	Double "c" in vaccine.
Wierd	Weird	"Weird" breaks the "i before e" rule.
Peirce	Pierce	"i" before "e" except after "c."
Concieve	Conceive	"i" before "e" except after "c."
Deceive	Deceive	"i" before "e" except after "c."
Percieve	Perceive	"i" before "e" except after "c."
Reciept	Receipt	"i" before "e" except after "c."
Retrive	Retrieve	"i" before "e" except after "c."
Seperate	Separate	"Separate" has "a" in the middle.

Words with Silent Letters :

These words have letters you don't pronounce, making them hard to spell correctly.

Incorrect Spelling	Correct Spelling	Trick to Remember
Acomplish	Accomplish	The word "accomplish" has a "c" – think of "accomplished" with a "c."
Govenor	Governor	Remember that "governor" has "nor" – think of a "governor" in "NOR"thern regions.
Humerus	Humorous	The word "humorous" has "humor" in it – think of being "full of humor."
Apropos	Appropriate	"Appropriate" has "appropriate" as it means "right" or "suitable."
Resign	Re-sign	Remember "re-sign" like signing again – it's not a silent letter but a different meaning.
Plumb	Plum	"Plum" is without the "b" – think of a "plum" in a "plum" tree.
Buisness	Business	The word "business" has "iness" – think of it as "busy-ness."
Writen	Written	"Written" has double "t" – think of writing with a double "t."
Knaw	Know	"Know" has a silent "k" – think of knowing without "k."
Acknowledge	Acknowledge	Remember that "acknowledge" has the "know" in it, so no extra "k."
Trule	True	"True" has no "l" – think of "truth" without the "l."
Tounge	Tongue	"Tongue" has "gue" – imagine "tongue" as "a game" with "gue."
Misinformation	Misinformation	The word "misinformation" has a "silent" "i" in the middle – "misinformation" flows with "silent i."
Asthma	Asthma	The "th" in "asthma" is pronounced – remember the "th" is silent.
Athelete	Athlete	"Athlete" has no extra "e" – think of an "athlete" as an "athl" with "e."
Unnecessary	Unnecessary	The word "unnecessary" has extra "s" – think of needing "no extra s."
Heir	Heir	"Heir" has a silent "h" – think of inheriting with no "h."
Subtle	Subtle	"Subtle" has a silent "b" – think of "subtle" as "not loud."
Debut	Debut	"Debut" has no "e" after "b" – think of it as "a debut" without the extra "e."
Faint	Faint	"Faint" has no "g" – think of a fainting feeling with no "g."

Trivia Corner

Here are examples of how spelling mistakes can change the entire meaning of a conversation

"Bare" vs. "Bear":
- Incorrect: "I saw a bare in the woods."
- Correct: "I saw a bear in the woods."
- Impact: A mix-up between seeing a naked person and seeing a wild animal.

"Principle" vs. "Principal":
- Incorrect: "The principle called me to his office."
- Correct: "The principal called me to his office."
- Impact: Confusing a fundamental truth with the head of a school.

"Accept" vs. "Except":
- Incorrect: "I except your apology."
- Correct: "I accept your apology."
- Impact: Suggesting exclusion instead of acceptance.

"Then" vs. "Than":
- Incorrect: "She is taller then me."
- Correct: "She is taller than me."
- Impact: Confusing a time sequence with a comparison.

"Compliment" vs. "Complement":
- Incorrect: "Your shoes really compliment your outfit."
- Correct: "Your shoes really complement your outfit."
- Impact: Confusing praise with something that completes.

"Desert" vs. "Dessert":
- Incorrect: "I love eating desert after dinner."
- Correct: "I love eating dessert after dinner."
- Impact: Mixing up a dry, sandy place with a sweet treat.

"Affect" vs. "Effect":
- Incorrect: "The weather can effect my mood."
- Correct: "The weather can affect my mood."
- Impact: Confusing the verb (influence) with the noun (result).

Trivia Corner

"Advice" vs. "Advise":
- Incorrect: "Can you give me some advise?"
- Correct: "Can you give me some advice?"
- Impact: Mixing up the noun (guidance) with the verb (to give guidance).

"Stationary" vs. "Stationery":
- Incorrect: "I bought some new stationary for school."
- Correct: "I bought some new stationery for school."
- Impact: Confusing something unmoving with writing supplies.

"Their" vs. "There" vs. "They're":
- Incorrect: "Their going to the park over they're."
- Correct: "They're going to the park over there."
- Impact: Confusing possession, location, and a contraction for "they are."

"Lose" vs. "Loose":
- Incorrect: "I always loose my keys."
- Correct: "I always lose my keys."
- Impact: Confusing the act of misplacing something with something not tight or fixed.

"Peace" vs. "Piece":
- Incorrect: "I want a piece of mind."
- Correct: "I want peace of mind."
- Impact: Confusing a state of tranquility with a part of something.

"Weather" vs. "Whether":
- Incorrect: "I'm not sure weather I'll go."
- Correct: "I'm not sure whether I'll go."
- Impact: Confusing atmospheric conditions with a conjunction indicating choice.

"Sight" vs. "Site" vs. "Cite":
- Incorrect: "I need to site my sources."
- Correct: "I need to cite my sources."
- Impact: Confusing the act of referencing with a location or a visual perception.

"Aloud" vs. "Allowed":
- Incorrect: "Is it aloud to talk in here?"
- Correct: "Is it allowed to talk in here?"
- Impact: Confusing the act of speaking loudly with being permitted to do something

ACTIVITY CORNER 9

Activity 1: Homophone Match-Up

Instructions: Create a matching game where students match homophones with their correct meanings.

1. Match the homophone **"there"** with its definition.
2. Match the homophone **"their"** with its definition.
3. Match the homophone **"they're"** with its definition.
4. Match the homophone **"to"** with its definition.
5. Match the homophone **"too"** with its definition.

Activity 2: Spelling Mistake Hunt

Instructions: Conduct a relay race where students correct sentences with common spelling mistakes.

1. I will definately go to the party.
2. She is a very inteligent student.
3. Please seperate the laundry into different piles.
4. He recieved a gift from his friend.
5. It is necessary to bring your own stationary.
6. The accomodations were very comfortable.
7. She was embarassed by her mistake.
8. The wierd noise scared the children.
9. He doesn't know wether to laugh or cry.
10. I recieved an invitation to the event.

10. Acing the Vocabulary Game in Exam

In this chapter, we will explore techniques to help you accurately guess the meaning of a word from four options in an English exam. These strategies are designed to improve your confidence and accuracy when dealing with challenging vocabulary questions.

Techniques for Guessing the Correct Meaning

1. Use Context Clues:

Definition:
Context clues are hints found within the surrounding text that can help you determine the meaning of an unfamiliar word.

Types of Context Clues:

(a) Definition Clue: The word's definition is directly stated.

- Example: "Arboreal animals, such as squirrels and monkeys, live in trees."
  Arboreal: related to trees.

(b) Synonym Clue: A synonym of the word is provided nearby.

- Example: "The book was so riveting, so captivating, that I couldn't put it down."
  Riveting: captivating.

(c) Antonym Clue: An antonym or a word with the opposite meaning is given.

- Example: "Unlike his gregarious sister, Tim was very shy and reserved."
  Gregarious: sociable.

(d) Example Clue: Examples are given to clarify the word.

- Example: "Celestial bodies, like stars, planets, and comets, can be seen with a telescope."
  Celestial: related to the sky or outer space.

2. Analyze Word Parts (Morphology):

Definition:
Analyzing word parts involves breaking down a word into its prefixes, root words, and suffixes to understand its meaning.

Word Parts:

(a) Prefixes: The beginning of a word.
Example: "Unhappy" (prefix "un-" means "not").

(b) Suffixes: The end of a word.
- Example: "Happiness" (suffix "-ness" indicates a state of being).
  -ness: state of being

(c) Root Words: The main part of the word.

- Example: "Biology" (root "bio" means "life").
  Bio: life

3. Eliminate Incorrect Options :

Definition:
Elimination involves crossing out incorrect options, thereby narrowing down the choices.

Practice:

Sentence: "Her meticulous attention to detail impressed everyone." Options:
1. Careless
2. Thorough
3. Quick
4. Inattentive

Elimination:

- "Careless" and "Inattentive" are opposites of what would impress.
- "Quick" does not fit with attention to detail.

Correct Answer: 2. Thorough

4. Use Word Familiarity :

Definition:

Using word familiarity involves recognizing similar words you know to help understand the meaning of an unfamiliar word.

Practice:

Word: "Benevolent" Options:

1. Kind
2. Cruel
3. Ignorant
4. Unaware

Familiarity: "Bene-" suggests something positive (like "benefit").

Correct Answer: 1. Kind

5 . Check for Logical Fit :

Definition:
Substituting each option into the sentence to see which makes the most sense.

Practice:

Sentence: "The scientist's postulate was groundbreaking."

Options:

1. Theory
2. Experiment
3. Observation
4. Measurement

Logical Fit:
- Substitute each option into the sentence.

Correct Answer: 1. Theory

6. Consider Connotations :

Definition:

Determining whether the word has a positive or negative connotation and matching it to the sentence's tone.

Practice:

Sentence: "The ominous clouds signaled a storm was coming."

Options:
1. Cheerful
2. Bright
3. Threatening
4. Clear

Connotation:
- "Ominous" suggests something negative or threatening.

Correct Answer: 3. Threatening

Conclusion

Mastering these techniques will help you confidently tackle vocabulary questions on your English exams. Practice regularly, use context clues, analyze word parts, eliminate incorrect options, rely on word familiarity, check for logical fit, and consider connotations. With these strategies, you'll be well-prepared to ace the vocabulary game in any exam.

Tables and Visual Aids
Common Prefixes, Suffixes, and Roots

Prefix	Meaning	Example	Meaning of Example
Un-	Not	Unhappy	Not happy
Pre-	Before	Predict	Say before
Dis-	Opposite of	Disagree	Opposite of agree

Suffix	Meaning	Example	Meaning of Example
-ful	Full of	Joyful	Full of joy
-less	Without	Hopeless	Without hope
-tion	State of	Celebration	State of celebrating

Root	Meaning	Example	Meaning of Example
Bio	Life	Biology	Study of life
Phil	Love	Philosophy	Love of wisdom
Chron	Time	Chronology	Study of time sequences

Common Context Clues

Type	Description	Example Sentence	Clue
Definition Clue	The word's definition is directly stated.	Arboreal animals, such as squirrels and monkeys, live in trees.	Arboreal: related to trees
Synonym Clue	A synonym is provided nearby.	The book was so riveting, so captivating, that I couldn't put it down.	Riveting: captivating
Antonym Clue	An antonym or a word with the opposite meaning is given.	Unlike his gregarious sister, Tim was very shy and reserved.	Gregarious: sociable
Example Clue	Examples clarify the word.	Celestial bodies, like stars, planets, and comets, can be seen with a telescope.	Celestial: related to the sky or outer space

Trivia Corner

- "Algebra" Origin: The word "algebra" comes from the Arabic word "al-jabr," which means "reunion of broken parts." It was introduced to Europe through the works of Persian mathematician Al-Khwarizmi.

- "Sarcasm" Roots: The word "sarcasm" comes from the Greek word "sarkazein," which means "to tear flesh like dogs." It's fitting for a form of speech that can be quite biting!

- "Ketchup" History: The word "ketchup" has its origins in the Chinese word "ke-tsiap," a type of fermented fish sauce. The condiment we know today has changed quite a bit from its original form.

- "Berserk" Backstory: The word "berserk" comes from Old Norse "berserkr," referring to Norse warriors who fought in a frenzied, wild state. They were said to wear bear skins, hence the name.

- "Robot" Revelation: The term "robot" was first used in a 1920 play by Czech writer Karel Čapek. It comes from the Czech word "robota," which means "forced labor" or "drudgery."

- "Avatar" Ascends: The word "avatar" comes from the Sanskrit "avatāra," which means "descent." In Hindu mythology, it refers to the descent of a deity to Earth, and in modern usage, it refers to a digital representation of a user.

- "Juggernaut" Journey: The word "juggernaut" originates from the Sanskrit "Jagannatha," a title of the Hindu god Vishnu, meaning "Lord of the Universe." It was used to describe the massive chariots in the deity's annual procession, which were said to crush anything in their path.

- "Karma" Deeds: "Karma" comes from the Sanskrit word "karma," which means "action" or "deed." In Hinduism and Buddhism, it refers to the idea that a person's actions determine their future fate.

- "Nirvana" Bliss: The word "nirvana" is derived from the Sanskrit "nirvāṇa," which means "blowing out" or "extinguishing." Buddhism signifies the ultimate state of liberation and freedom from suffering.

- "Salary" and Salt: The word "salary" comes from the Latin "salarium," which was a payment made to Roman soldiers for the purchase of salt. Salt was a valuable commodity at the time.

ACTIVITY CORNER 10

Activity 1: Guess the correct meaning of the word

1. Use context clues to determine the meaning of "gregarious" in the following sentence. Sentence: "Unlike his gregarious sister, Tim was very shy and reserved."

   1. Shy
   2. Outgoing
   3. Angry
   4. Sad

2: Analyze the word parts of "antipathy."

   1. Sympathy
   2. Love
   3. Dislike
   4. Attraction

3: Eliminate incorrect options for "cognizant."
Sentence: "She was not cognizant of the risks involved."

   1. Aware
   2. Ignorant
   3. Uninformed
   4. Unaware

4. Use word familiarity to guess the meaning of "audible." Options:
   1. Visible
   2. Hearable
   3. Touchable
   4. Tastable

5: Check for logical fit for "lucid." Sentence: "The professor's explanation was lucid and easy to understand."

   1. Confusing
   2. Clear
   3. Difficult
   4. Ambiguous

ACTIVITY ANSWERS

83

ACTIVITY CORNER 1

1. Spelling Test: Correct spelling of the given words:

1. Accommodation
2. Necessary
3. Environment
4. Definitely
5. Recommend
6. Embarrassment
7. Maintenance
8. Rhythm
9. Separate
10. Occurrence

2. Vocabulary Test: Match the words with their correct definitions:

1. Exacerbate: (b) To worsen
2. Benevolent: (a) Kind-hearted
3. Ambiguous: (b) Vague
4. Persevere: (b) To continue
5. Candid: (b) Honest

ACTIVITY CORNER 2

Answers:

1. B) Context clues
2. B) Intermediate
3. D) Consider
4. B) Un-
5. B) -ful
6. C) Sociable
7. C) Magnanimous
8. D) Definition clue
9. A) Joy and -ful
10. B) Ignoring surrounding text

84

ACTIVITY CORNER 3

EXERCISE 1: FILL IN THE BLANKS WITH THE CORRECT SPELLING

Solution of Exercise 1:
1. children
2. making
3. received
4. play
5. biggest

Solution of Exercise 2:
1. C) running
2. B) noticed
3. B) happiness
4. A) believe

Activity Corner 3: Spelling Bee Practice

Sample Word List:
- Eloquent
- Magnanimous
- Perseverance
- Inconspicuous
- Phenomenon
- Superfluous
- Zephyr
- Querulous
- Ambiguous
- Tenacity
- Infallible
- Conspicuous
- Serendipity
- Ubiquitous
- Effervescent
- Gregarious

Sample Word List:
- Perfunctory
- Obfuscate
- Soliloquy
- Onomatopoeia

ACTIVITY CORNER 4

FILL-IN-THE-BLANKS

Answers:
1. Elated
2. Cowered
3. Voracious
4. Tumultuous
5. Bewildering
6. Arboretum

Multiple Choice Quiz

Answers:
1. c) Elated
2. a) Voracious
3. b) Confusing or puzzling
4. c) Stormy or chaotic
5. a) Crouched down in fear

Match the Following

Answers:
1. b) Furious
2. d) Fast
3. a) Bright
4. c) Decrease
5. e) Sad

ACTIVITY CORNER 5

Activity 1: Multiple Choice Questions

1. c) Decreased retention of information
2. d) All of the above
3. b) Using a vocabulary notebook
4. b) It reinforces pronunciation and retention
5. c) Incidental learning

Activity 2: Match the Words with Their Definitions

1. b) A story, poem, or picture that can be interpreted to reveal a hidden meaning
2. a) A long speech by a character alone on stage
3. e) A figure of speech that involves an implied comparison
4. d) An exaggerated statement or claim not meant to be taken literally
5. c) The expression of one's meaning by using language that normally signifies the opposite

Activity 3: True or False

1. False
2. False
3. False
4. True
5. True

Activity 4: Fill in the Blanks

1. vocabulary
2. context
3. pronunciation
4. vocabulary notebook
5. review

ACTIVITY CORNER 6

ACTIVITY 1: IDENTIFY THE ROOT

Answer:

1. Audible: audi (hear)
2. Biology: bio (life)
3. Predict: dict (speak)
4. Transportation: port (carry)
5. Television: vis (see)
6. Dermatology: derm (skin)
7. Submarine: marine (sea)
8. Hydration: hydr (water)
9. Manuscript: script (write)
10. Astronaut: astro (star)

ACTIVITY 2 : MATCHING PREFIXES AND SUFFIXES

Answer:

1. Anti- b) Against
2. Dis- d) Not
3. -ful e) Full of
4. -less c) Without
5. Pre- a) Before
6. Sub- f) Under/Below
7. -ment g) Action/Process
8. -ness h) State of
9. -ive i) Having the nature of
10. Inter- j) Between

ACTIVITY 3 : MATCHING PREFIXES AND SUFFIXES

- Un- + known = unknown
- Inter- + national = international
- Care + -ful = careful
- Happy + -ness = happiness
- Celebrate + -tion = celebration
- Danger + -ous = dangerous
- Write + -ive = creative
- Geology + -ist = geologist
- Joy + -ous = joyous
- Comfort + -able = comfortable

ACTIVITY 4 : CREATE YOUR OWN WORD TREE

```
            geo
           / | \
geography geology geothermal
     /      |         \
Geography  Geology   Geothermal energy
is the study  studies   comes from the
of the earth. the earth. heat of the earth.
```

```
            scrib
           / | \
   describe inscribe scribble
      /       |        \
Describe your Inscribe your Don't scribble
favorite book name on the  on your homework,
 in detail.   book cover.   keep it neat!
```

```
             tele
            / | \
   telephone television telescope
      /        |          \
Call your friend Watch your  See distant stars
   using the     favorite    through a
   telephone.   show on      telescope.
                television.
```

88

ACTIVITY CORNER 7

ACTIVITY 1: CORRECT SPELLING QUIZ

Answers:

1. b) Accommodate
2. a) Misunderstanding
3. c) Environmentally
4. c) Committee
5. c) Millennium

ACTIVITY 2 : MATCH THE FOLLOWING MNEMONICS

Answers:

1. Embarrassment - e) Emma Makes Bears And Rats Run Away Scared, Sometimes Emma Naps Too
2. Millennium - b) My Illogical Little Lizard Enjoys New Neat Ice-cream Under Moonlight
3. Guarantee - c) Giant Unicorns Always Run Around Never Tearing Everything Else
4. Entrepreneur - a) Every New Tree Reaches Exceptional Peaks, Realizing Every New Unique Resource
5. Committee - d) Cats Often Meet Mice In The Tea Room Eating Everything

ACTIVITY CORNER 8

ACTIVITY 1: VOCABULARY CHALLENGE: CHOOSE THE CORRECT WORD

Answer Key:
1. exciting
2. growth
3. development
4. participate
5. enhance
6. pursuing
7. volunteering
8. engage
9. vocabulary
10. improve
11. writing
12. exploring
13. enrich
14. proofread
15. common
16. advanced
17. persuasive
18. sounding
19. concise
20. expand
21. transform
22. exceptional

ACTIVITY 2: FIND THE ERRORS

Incorrect Spelling	Correct Spelling
crusial	crucial
oppurtunities	opportunities
grouth	growth
nuture	nurture
knoledge	knowledge
extracuricular	extracurricular
inritch	enrich
comunication	communication
sucsess	success
proofreed	proofread
tesaurus	thesaurus
synonims	synonyms
dilligant	diligent
brigt	bright

ACTIVITY CORNER 9

ACTIVITY 1 : HOMOPHONE MATCH-UP

Answers:

1. There - A location or place.
2. Their - Possessive form meaning "belonging to them."
3. They're - Contraction of "they are."
4. To - A preposition indicating direction.
5. Too - An adverb meaning "also" or "excessively."

ACTIVITY 2 : SPELLING MISTAKE HUNT

Answers:

1. I will definitely go to the party.
2. She is a very intelligent student.
3. Please separate the laundry into different piles.
4. He received a gift from his friend.
5. It is necessary to bring your own stationery.
6. The accommodations were very comfortable.
7. She was embarrassed by her mistake.
8. The weird noise scared the children.
9. He doesn't know whether to laugh or cry.
10. I received an invitation to the event.

ACTIVITY CORNER 10

ACTIVITY 1: GUESS THE CORRECT MEANING OF THE WORD

Answers:

1. Correct Answer: 2. Outgoing
2. Correct Answer: 3. Dislike
3. Correct Answer: 1. Aware
4. Correct Answer: 2. Hearable
5. Correct Answer: 2. Clear

11. Build Your Word Bank: Vocabulary Essentials

VOCABULARY IMPROVEMENT GROUPS

GROUP 1: WORDS FROM LATIN ROOTS

Word	Breakdown	Meaning	Tip to Remember	Similar Words
Amicable	Amic- (friend) + -able (able)	Friendly	Think "amicable" like "amiable"	Friendly, Cordial
Belligerent	Bell- (war) + -ent (quality of)	Hostile	"Bell" sounds like "battle"	Hostile, Aggressive
Benefactor	Bene- (good) + factor (doer)	One who helps others	"Bene" means good	Patron, Supporter
Malediction	Male- (bad) + -diction (speaking)	Curse	"Male" means bad, opposite of "bene"	Curse, Damnation
Magnanimous	Magn- (great) + animous (spirit)	Generous	"Magn" is great, think magnify	Generous, Noble
Veracity	Ver- (truth) + -acity (quality)	Truthfulness	"Ver" like verify, which means to confirm the truth	Honesty, Integrity
Precipitate	Pre- (before) + cipit- (headlong) + -ate (to cause)	Cause to happen suddenly	"Pre" means before, something happens suddenly	Trigger, Expedite
Incredulous	In- (not) + cred- (believe) + -ous (full of)	Skeptical	"Cred" means believe, "in" means not	Skeptical, Disbelieving
Equanimity	Equ- (equal) + anim- (mind) + -ity (state of)	Calmness	"Equ" means equal, balance of mind	Composure, Serenity
Obdurate	Ob- (against) + dur- (hard) + -ate (state)	Stubborn	"Dur" like durable, tough to change	Stubborn, Unyielding

VOCABULARY IMPROVEMENT GROUPS

GROUP 2: WORDS FROM GREEK ROOTS

Word	Breakdown	Meaning	Tip to Remember	Similar Words
Chronology	Chron- (time) + -logy (study of)	Study of time sequences	"Chron" as in chronological order	Timeline, Sequence
Democracy	Demo- (people) + -cracy (government)	Government by the people	"Demo" means people	Republic, Self-government
Philosophy	Philo- (love) + -sophy (wisdom)	Love of wisdom	"Philo" means love, "sophy" means wisdom	Wisdom, Thought
Autonomy	Auto- (self) + -nomy (law)	Self-governance	"Auto" means self, self-law	Independence, Sovereignty
Apathetic	A- (not) + path- (feeling) + -etic (quality)	Indifferent	"Path" means feeling, "a" means not	Indifferent, Uninterested
Kaleidoscope	Kaleido- (beautiful) + -scope (view)	A constantly changing pattern	"Kaleido" means beautiful, "scope" means view	Colorful, Pattern
Homogeneous	Homo- (same) + -geneous (kind)	Of the same kind	"Homo" means same	Uniform, Consistent
Hypothesis	Hypo- (under) + -thesis (proposition)	Proposed explanation	"Hypo" means under, "thesis" a proposition	Theory, Assumption
Metamorphosis	Meta- (change) + morph- (form) + -osis (process)	Transformation	"Meta" means change, "morph" means form	Transformation, Evolution
Bibliophile	Biblio- (book) + -phile (lover)	Book lover	"Biblio" means book, "phile" means lover	Bookworm, Reader

VOCABULARY IMPROVEMENT GROUPS

GROUP 3: WORDS WITH POSITIVE CONNOTATIONS

Word	Breakdown	Meaning	Tip to Remember	Similar Words
Benevolent	Bene- (good) + volent (wishing)	Kind-hearted	"Bene" means good	Kind, Charitable
Exuberant	Ex- (out) + uber (fruitful) + -ant (quality)	Joyfully energetic	"Ex" means out, overflowing with energy	Lively, Enthusiastic
Magnanimous	Magn- (great) + animous (spirit)	Generous	"Magn" means great, think magnify	Generous, Noble
Serendipity	Ser- (serene) + endipity (finding)	Finding happiness by chance	Think serene, happy discoveries	Luck, Fortuity
Jubilant	Jubil- (shout for joy) + -ant (quality)	Extremely joyful	"Jubil" sounds like jubilee	Joyful, Elated
Altruistic	Altru- (other) + -istic (quality)	Selflessly concerned for others	"Altru" sounds like alter, helping others	Selfless, Philanthropic
Felicitous	Felic- (happy) + -itous (full of)	Well-suited, pleasant	"Felic" sounds like felicity, happiness	Apt, Suitable
Ebullient	E- (out) + bulli- (boil) + -ent (quality)	Cheerfully enthusiastic	"Ebull" sounds like bubble, overflowing with joy	Bubbly, Cheerful
Amicable	Amic- (friend) + -able (able)	Friendly	Think "amicable" like "amiable"	Friendly, Cordial
Sanguine	Sanguin- (blood) + -e (quality)	Optimistic	"Sanguin" means blood, think red cheeks	Optimistic, Cheerful

VOCABULARY IMPROVEMENT GROUPS

GROUP 4: WORDS WITH NEGATIVE CONNOTATIONS

Word	Breakdown	Meaning	Tip to Remember	Similar Words
Malevolent	Male- (bad) + volent (wishing)	Evil-minded	"Male" means bad	Malicious, Spiteful
Ominous	Omin- (omen) + -ous (full of)	Threatening	"Omin" sounds like omen	Threatening, Sinister
Vindictive	Vindict- (revenge) + -ive (quality)	Revengeful	"Vindict" sounds like convict, seeking revenge	Revengeful, Bitter
Nefarious	Nefar- (evil) + -ious (full of)	Wicked	"Nefar" sounds like nefarious	Wicked, Evil
Pernicious	Per- (thoroughly) + nic- (harm) + -ious (full of)	Harmful	"Nic" sounds like noxious, harmful	Harmful, Destructive
Egregious	E- (out) + greg- (flock) + -ious (full of)	Outrageously bad	"Greg" means flock, standing out negatively	Outrageous, Shocking
Deleterious	Deleter- (harmful) + -ious (full of)	Harmful	"Delete" sounds like to remove, harmful effect	Harmful, Detrimental
Invidious	In- (against) + vid- (see) + -ious (full of)	Envious, causing ill will	"Invid" sounds like envy	Hateful, Resentful
Recalcitrant	Re- (back) + calcitr- (kicking) + -ant (quality)	Stubbornly resistant	"Calci" sounds like calcify, hardened	Uncooperative, Defiant
Insolent	In- (not) + solent (customary)	Disrespectful	"Sole" sounds like sole, standing alone in behavior	Disrespectful, Impudent

VOCABULARY IMPROVEMENT GROUPS

GROUP 5: ACADEMIC WORDS

Word	Breakdown	Meaning	Tip to Remember	Similar Words
Hypothesis	Hypo- (under) + -thesis (proposition)	Proposed explanation	"Hypo" means under, "thesis" a proposition	Theory, Assumption
Analyze	Ana- (up) + lyze (loosen)	Examine in detail	"Ana" means up, breaking up details	Examine, Evaluate
Synthesize	Syn- (together) + -thesize (put)	Combine	"Syn" means together, putting together	Combine, Integrate
Evaluate	E- (out) + valu- (worth) + -ate (to make)	Assess	"Valu" means worth, determining value	Assess, Judge
Interpret	Inter- (between) + pret (explain)	Explain the meaning	"Inter" means between, explaining connections	Explain, Clarify
Formulate	Form- (shape) + -ulate (make)	Create methodically	"Form" means shape, methodical creation	Create, Devise
Corroborate	Cor- (together) + robor- (strength) + -ate (to make)	Confirm	"Robor" means strength, confirming with strength	Confirm, Support
Conceptualize	Concept- (idea) + -ualize (to make)	Form a concept	"Concept" means idea, forming ideas	Envision, Imagine
Critique	Crit- (judge) + -ique (process)	Evaluate critically	"Crit" sounds like critic, evaluating	Review, Assess
Infer	In- (into) + fer- (carry)	Conclude from evidence	"Infer" means to deduce, think inference	Deduce, Conclude

97

MOST USED ROOT WORDS FROM DIFFERENT LANGUAGES

TABLE 1: LATIN ROOTS

Root	Meaning	Examples
Aqua	Water	Aquarium, Aquatic, Aqueduct
Aud	Hear	Audience, Audible, Auditory
Bene	Good	Benefit, Benevolent, Benefactor
Dict	Say, Speak	Dictate, Dictionary, Predict
Duc/Duct	Lead	Conduct, Induce, Educate
Form	Shape	Formation, Reform, Transform
Ject	Throw	Eject, Inject, Project
Port	Carry	Transport, Import, Portable
Rupt	Break	Interrupt, Erupt, Rupture
Spect	Look	Inspect, Spectator, Spectacle
Struct	Build	Construct, Structure, Destruction

TABLE 2: GREEK ROOTS

Root	Meaning	Examples
Chron	Time	Chronology, Synchronize, Chronic
Dem	People	Democracy, Demographic, Epidemic
Philo	Love	Philosophy, Philanthropy, Bibliophile
Auto	Self	Autonomy, Automobile, Autograph
Hypo	Under	Hypothesis, Hypodermic, Hypothermia
Morph	Form	Metamorphosis, Amorphous, Morphology
Therm	Heat	Thermal, Thermometer, Thermostat
Path	Feeling	Empathy, Apathy, Pathos
Bio	Life	Biology, Biography, Biodegradable
Geo	Earth	Geography, Geology, Geothermal

MOST USED ROOT WORDS FROM DIFFERENT LANGUAGES

TABLE 3: FRENCH AND SANSKRIT ROOTS

Root	Language	Meaning	Examples
Café	French	Coffee	Café, Cafeteria
Château	French	Castle	Château, Chatelaine
Ballet	French	Dance	Ballet, Ballerina
Avatar	Sanskrit	Descent	Avatar, Avatara
Karma	Sanskrit	Action	Karma, Karmic
Nirvana	Sanskrit	Liberation	Nirvana, Nirvanic
Yoga	Sanskrit	Union	Yoga, Yogi
Guru	Sanskrit	Teacher	Guru, Gurukula
Mantra	Sanskrit	Sacred Utterance	Mantra, Mantric
Chakra	Sanskrit	Wheel, Energy Center	Chakra, Chakric

TABLE 4 : GERMAN ROOTS

Root	Meaning	Examples
Zeit	Time	Zeitgeist, Zeitgeber
Kinder	Children	Kindergarten, Kindergeld
Haus	House	House, Hausfrau
Arbeit	Work	Arbeit, Arbeitskraft
Geist	Spirit, Mind	Zeitgeist, Poltergeist
Sturm	Storm	Sturm und Drang, Stormtrooper
Wald	Forest	Walden, Waldheim

TABLE 5 : OLD ENGLISH ROOTS

Root	Meaning	Examples
Cyning	King	King, Kingdom
Mann	Person, Human	Man, Woman, Mankind
Hús	House	House, Husband
Frēond	Friend	Friend, Friendship
Folc	People	Folk, Folklore
Scip	Ship	Ship, Skipper

MOST USED ROOT WORDS FROM DIFFERENT LANGUAGES

TABLE 3: FRENCH AND SANSKRIT ROOTS

Root	Language	Meaning	Examples
Café	French	Coffee	Café, Cafeteria
Château	French	Castle	Château, Chatelaine
Ballet	French	Dance	Ballet, Ballerina
Avatar	Sanskrit	Descent	Avatar, Avatara
Karma	Sanskrit	Action	Karma, Karmic
Nirvana	Sanskrit	Liberation	Nirvana, Nirvanic
Yoga	Sanskrit	Union	Yoga, Yogi
Guru	Sanskrit	Teacher	Guru, Gurukula
Mantra	Sanskrit	Sacred Utterance	Mantra, Mantric
Chakra	Sanskrit	Wheel, Energy Center	Chakra, Chakric

TABLE 4 : GERMAN ROOTS

Root	Meaning	Examples
Zeit	Time	Zeitgeist, Zeitgeber
Kinder	Children	Kindergarten, Kindergeld
Haus	House	House, Hausfrau
Arbeit	Work	Arbeit, Arbeitskraft
Geist	Spirit, Mind	Zeitgeist, Poltergeist
Sturm	Storm	Sturm und Drang, Stormtrooper
Wald	Forest	Walden, Waldheim

12. Most Misspelled Words & Tricks to Remember

MOST MISSPELLED WORDS BY HIGH SCHOOL STUDENTS

Word	Common Misspelling	Trick to Remember
Accommodate	Acommodate, Accomodate	Remember it has "two c's" and "two m's"
Definitely	Definately	It has "finite" in it, like "definite"
Separate	Seperate	There is "a rat" in "separate"
Necessary	Neccessary, Necesary	One collar (c) and two socks (s)
Occurrence	Occurence, Ocurrence	Two c's, two r's in "occurrence"
Calendar	Calender	"Calendar" has "ar" at the end, like in "arm"
Embarrass	Embarass, Embarras	Two r's and two s's – think "embarrassment"
Recommend	Reccomend, Recomend	It has "two m's" – "re-commend"
Privilege	Privlege, Privelege	Remember the "i" before the "lege"
A lot	Alot	Always two words: "a lot"
Liaison	Laison, Liason	Remember the "i" before "a" and after "a"
Existence	Existance	"Exist" ends in "ence," not "ance"
Jewelry	Jewerly	"Jew" + "el" + "ry"
License	Lisense, Lisence	Ends with "ense," not "ence"
Questionnaire	Questionaire	It has "two n's" like in "questioning"
Perseverance	Perserverance	"Persevere" + "ance"
Convenient	Conveniant	Ends with "ent," not "ant"
Rhythm	Rytm, Rhythmn	No vowels between "rh" and "thm"
Broccoli	Brocoli, Broccli	Two c's and one l
Conscience	Concience, Conscence	"Con" + "science"
Playwright	Playwrite, Playrite	"Wright" means builder
Receipt	Reciept	"E" before "I" after "C"
Conscious	Concious, Conscous	"Con" + "sci" + "ous"
Supersede	Supercede	"Sede" like "cede"
Maintenance	Maintainance	"Maintain" + "ance"
Vacuum	Vacume, Vaccum	Two u's, one c
Misspell	Mispell, Misspel	Double "s" in "miss"
Cemetery	Cemetary	"E" in every syllable
Millennium	Millenium, Milennium	Two l's and two n's
Entrepreneur	Entreprenur, Entrepenuer	"Entre" + "pre" + "neur"
Questionnaire	Questionaire	It has "two n's" like in "questioning"
Occasion	Ocassion, Occaision	Two c's and one s
Threshold	Threshhold, Threshhold	Only one "h" after "s"
Mischievous	Mischevious, Mischeivous	"Mischief" + "ous"
Desperate	Desparate	Ends with "ate," not "ate"
Noticeable	Noticable	Keep the "e" after "c"

Word	Common Misspelling	Trick to Remember
Acquaintance	Acquantance, Acquintance	"Acquaint" + "ance"
Guarantee	Guarentee, Guarantie	"Guaran" + "tee"
Relevant	Revelant, Relevent	"Ant" at the end, not "ent"
Occasion	Ocassion, Occaision	Two c's and one s
Recommend	Reccomend, Recomend	It has "two m's" – "re-commend"
Bureaucracy	Beaurocracy, Bureaucrcy	"Bureau" + "cracy"
Maneuver	Manuever, Maneuver	"Man" + "euver"
Acquiesce	Aquisce, Acquiesse	"Acqui" + "esce"
Occasionally	Ocassionally, Occassionally	"Occasion" + "ally"
Pronunciation	Pronouciation	"Pronounce" becomes "pronunciation"
Noticeable	Noticable	Keep the "e" after "c"
Calendar	Calender	"Calendar" has "ar" at the end, like in "arm"
Knowledge	Knowlege, Knoledge	"Know" + "ledge"
Government	Goverment, Govenment	"Govern" + "ment"

We'd Love Your Feedback!

⭐ ⭐ ⭐ ⭐ ⭐

Please let us know how we're doing by leaving us a review.

CONCLUSION

Congratulations on finishing the High School Spelling and Vocabulary Workbook! This program is designed to provide you with the tools and strategies necessary to improve your spelling and vocabulary skills, which are crucial for academic achievement.

In this workbook, you have examined the origins of words, addressed common spelling mistakes, and completed various interactive exercises designed to enhance your understanding and memory. By mastering these aspects, you are preparing for exams and establishing a solid base for effective communication in all aspects of life.

Key Takeaways:

- **Understanding Roots and Origins**: Learning word origins can help with meanings and spellings.
- **Common Spelling Mistakes**: Practice commonly misspelled words to improve accuracy.
- **Interactive Exercises**: Use workbook activities for memory retention and skill application.
- **Techniques for Exam Success**: Strategies for guessing word meanings and breaking down complex terms.

Moving Forward:

The skills in this workbook are not just for passing exams; they are lifelong assets. Strong spelling and vocabulary skills will serve you well in college, in your career, and your daily life. Remember that language is a powerful tool that can open doors to new opportunities and help you express yourself clearly and confidently.

Final Tip:

"Make reading a habit. It's the best way to expand your vocabulary and reinforce spelling. Look up unfamiliar words and use new ones in writing and conversations. Keep working hard and striving for excellence. Best of luck on your academic journey!"

APPENDIX- 1 : ADDITIONAL RESOURCES

Recommended Books

Title	Author	Description
Word Power Made Easy	Norman Lewis	A comprehensive vocabulary-building book.
The Elements of Style	Strunk and White	A classic guide to effective writing and grammar.
Vocabulary for the High School Student	Harold Levine, Norman Levine, and Robert T. Levine	A book focused on vocabulary development for high school students.
The Vocabulary Builder Workbook	Chris Lele	Engaging activities and exercises for vocabulary growth.
Webster's New World Essential Vocabulary	David A Herzog	A guide to expanding your vocabulary with essential words.

Recommended Websites

Website	URL	Description
Merriam-Webster Dictionary	www.merriam-webster.com	Online dictionary and thesaurus with word games and quizzes.
Vocabulary.com	www.vocabulary.com	Personalized vocabulary practice and games.
Quizlet	www.quizlet.com	Flashcards and learning tools for various subjects, including vocabulary.
Grammarly Blog	www.grammarly.com/blog	Articles on writing, grammar, and vocabulary improvement.
BBC Learning English	www.bbc.co.uk/learningenglish	English language learning resources and vocabulary exercises.

APPENDIX- 1 : ADDITIONAL RESOURCES

Recommended Apps

App	Platform	Description
Duolingo	iOS, Android	Language learning app with vocabulary practice.
Anki	iOS, Android	Flashcard app that helps with memorization.
Memrise	iOS, Android	Language and vocabulary learning app with interactive courses.
WordUp Vocabulary	iOS, Android	App that helps you learn new words through games and quizzes.
Vocabulary.com	iOS, Android	App version of the website with personalized vocabulary practice.

We'd Love Your Feedback!

★ ★ ★ ★ ★

Please let us know how we're doing by leaving us a review.

APPENDIX- 2 : WRITING PROMPTS TO USE NEW VOCABULARY IN CONTEXT

Prompt	Description
Describe Your Ideal Day	Use at least five new vocabulary words to describe what your perfect day would look like. Be detailed in your descriptions to make the reader visualize your experience.
A Memorable Event	Write about a memorable event in your life. Incorporate at least five vocabulary words from the workbook to enhance your narrative.
Persuasive Essay	Choose a topic you are passionate about and write a persuasive essay using at least seven new vocabulary words to strengthen your argument. Possible topics include environmental issues, school policies, or technological advancements.
Create a Short Story	Craft a short story of at least 500 words using at least ten new vocabulary words. Your story can be about anything you like – mystery, adventure, fantasy, or a day in the life of a student.
Letter to a Friend	Write a letter to a friend explaining something you've recently learned or experienced. Use at least five vocabulary words from the workbook to make your letter more engaging and informative.
Debate Preparation	Prepare for a debate on a current issue. Write a paragraph for your opening statement using at least five new vocabulary words. Ensure your argument is clear and compelling.
News Article	Imagine you are a journalist. Write a news article about a recent event or a topic of interest. Use at least seven new vocabulary words to make your reporting precise and professional.
Descriptive Paragraph	Write a descriptive paragraph about a place you have visited or would like to visit. Use at least five new vocabulary words to help your reader visualize the scene.
Poem or Song Lyrics	Create a poem or song lyrics using at least five new vocabulary words. Focus on how the words contribute to the imagery and emotion you want to convey.
Future Goals	Write about your future goals and aspirations. Use at least five new vocabulary words to articulate your ambitions and how you plan to achieve them.

YOUNG WRITER SERIES - DR. FANATOMY

Made in the USA
Columbia, SC
15 April 2025